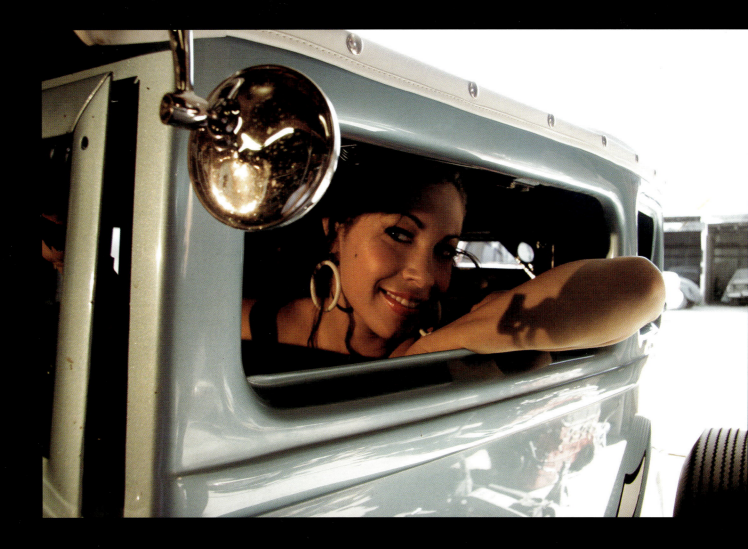

hot rod pin-ups II

Gearhead Girls and Dragstrip Dolls

DAVID PERRY

Foreword by COOP

DEDICATED TO WALTER COTTEN

First published in 2008 by Motorbooks, an imprint of MBI Publishing Company, 400 First Avenue North, Suite 300, Minneapolis, MN 55401 USA

Motorbooks titles are also available at discounts in bulk quantity for industrial or sales-promotional use. For details write to Special Sales Manager at MBI Publishing Company, 400 First Avenue North, Suite 300, Minneapolis, MN 55401 USA.

To find out more about our books, join us online at www.motorbooks.com.

Library of Congress Cataloging-in-Publication Data
Perry, David, 1959-
  Hot rod pin-ups II : gearhead girls and dragstrip dolls / David Perry.
    p. cm.
  Includes index.
  ISBN: 978-0-7603-3171-2 (hb w/ jkt)
  1. Glamour photography. 2. Photography of women. 3. Hot rods—Pictorial works. 4. Pinup art--United States. I. Title.

TR678.P4432 2005
779'.24--dc22

2008009012

Editorial: Dennis Pernu
Design: Suzi Hutsell

Printed in China

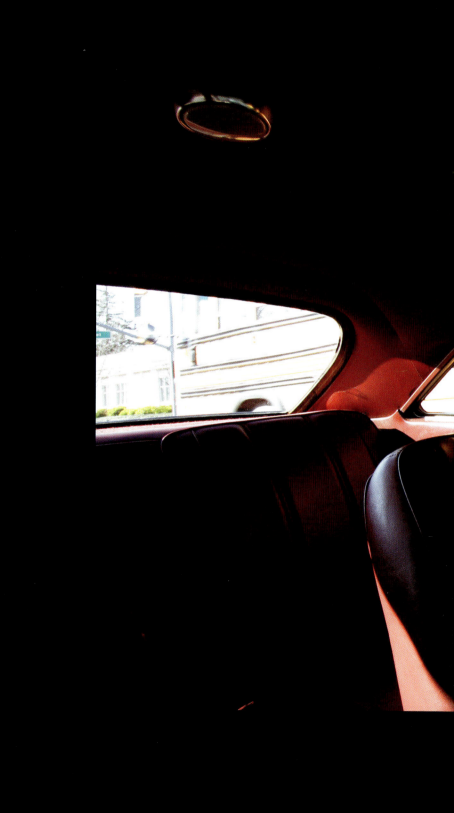

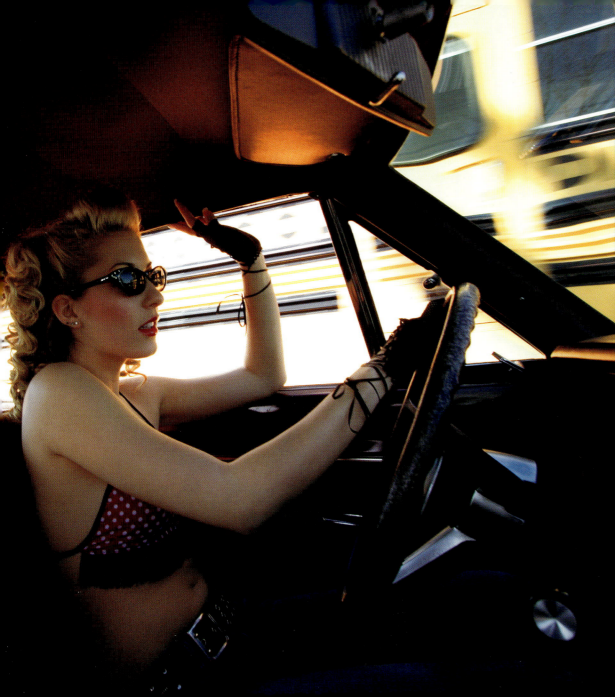

contents

NOTHIN'...'CEPT FOR CARS AND GIRLS:
OBJECTS OF DESIRE IN THE MIND OF THE VIEWER

BY COOP

"Just write something about hot rods and girls."

Sounds easy enough, but where do you start?

When I was a child, the first thing I started to draw was cars. Inspired by Hot Wheels, Evel Knievel, and *Speed Racer* cartoons, I filled innumerable Big Chief tablets with drawing after drawing of racecars and dragsters, each festooned with more chrome pipes and hood scoops than the last. I got my first taste of notoriety by being the kid in first grade who could draw the cool cars.

Fast forward a few years, and as is usually the case, little boys begin to notice the opposite sex. I decided I would turn my automotive-rendering talents to the study of the female form. I soon ended up in the principal's office, the flustered nincompoop behind the desk doing his best to scare the hell out of a ten-year-old as he called my father to bring down the hammer of doom on my perverted head. To his credit, my pop laughed at the busybody bureaucrat, and I was not punished for my first effort at delineating the feminine physique. I didn't know it then, but I had found my calling.

So cars and girls became linked in my mind at a very early age. It didn't hurt that I was growing up during the mutton-chopped glory days of drag racing and American motorsport, when every belch of fiery nitro was accompanied by a beautiful girl showing off what the good Lord gave her. Jungle Pam and Linda Vaughn were just as spectacular and bodacious as the metalflake floppers and fiery Top Fuelers that roared and zoomed past their heavenly bodies.

So what's the connection?

"We affirm that the world's magnificence has been enriched by a new beauty: the beauty of speed. A racing car whose hood is adorned with great pipes, like serpents of explosive breath—a roaring car that seems to ride on grapeshot is more beautiful than the Victory of Samothrace." **—Marinetti, "Manifesto of Futurism"**

The female form has been a primary inspiration for artists since, well, since there was art. About 25,000 years ago, some hairy fellow carved a curvy little number that we now know as the Venus of Willendorf, and ever since, Art has just been an excuse to talk some lovely creature into shedding her garments in the name of the muse. The ancient Greeks, the Romans, the Renaissance, the Academic painters of the eighteenth and nineteenth centuries, it was all about the ladies. (Well, maybe some other stuff too, like allegory and myth, and painting Bible stories for those high rollers in the Vatican, but that's another story.)

Then, just around the beginning of the twentieth century, a fellow named Gottlieb Daimler got the bright idea to attach a motor to a carriage.

Less than ten years later, an Italian poet, Filippo Tommaso Marinetti, wrote the "Manifesto of Futurism," an artistic statement of purpose that disposed of past outmoded ideals of beauty, replacing them with a modern aesthetic that worshipped technology, novelty, and, most of all, speed. The Futurists loved their racecars.

Now the Fururists were a screwy bunch, and most of them turned into fascists when Mussolini came to power, but they were the first artists to appreciate the pure aesthetics of the automobile, the first to see a mechanical, man-made object every bit as beautiful as anything found in nature. To this day, anybody who paints a hot rod or shoots a photo of a metalflake custom Merc owes a debt to the Futurists.

So where am I going with all this? We have thousands of years of Western culture defined by the worship of the feminine form in art running headlong into the novelty of chrome and speed, the essence of modernity. These two trains of thought were bound to collide, and they finally did, with a little help from that American symbol of ingenuity, the hot rod.

"There's nothin' else in this whole wide world, 'cept for cars and girls." —**The Dictators, "I Live for Cars and Girls"**

Hot rodding, along with baseball and jazz, are America's unique contributions to world culture. As soon as Americans got their collective mitts on Henry Ford's cheap and reliable Model T, they began to tear it apart. Anything that could be done to make a jalopy go faster, somebody figured out a way to do it, and somebody else copied it and made it better. Along the way, careers were begun, industries were invented, heroes were made, and a culture was born.

One of the innovators who made his fortune out on the dry lakebeds was Robert E. Petersen. In 1948 he began publishing *Hot Rod* magazine. The first few issues were a little thin on content, but it was the beginning of a publishing empire that lives on today. One of the features in the earliest issues of *Hot Rod* was called "Parts with Appeal." It was a full-page photo of a lovely young lady holding a piece of speed equipment, usually something manufactured by one of the advertisers in the back pages of the magazine.

Up to this point there was already a history of "trophy girls" at the racetrack posing next to a grinning, oil-soaked driver in the winners' circle. It was a small conceptual leap from the commemorative photos taken at these events to simply shooting the girl with the car, minus driver. However, those first "Parts with Appeal" photos reached a level of abstraction. Something new was created. It wasn't just a car on display with the girl—it was just a part of a car, something that was utilitarian and functional. By presenting it with a beautiful woman, the part was allowed to be beautiful, to be fetishized. This was something new. The link between cars and girls was complete.

Sixty years later, this link is so taken for granted it is hard even to imagine that it was ever a novelty. Automobiles are fetishized and sexualized like nothing else in American culture. Guys in high school build cars to attract girls, but in many ways the car becomes a substitute for the female, an object that is coveted, pampered, and adored until it seems to have a life of its own. (Do I even have to point out how many men give their car a woman's name?) It is taken for granted that cars are beautiful, sexy and thrilling, in the same way that a woman would be considered beautiful, sexy, and thrilling.

So here we are, looking at a book of David Perry's amazing photographs of beautiful women and beautiful automobiles, both objects of desire in the mind of the viewer. It's not even a little weird.

Culture is a wonderful thing, ain't it?

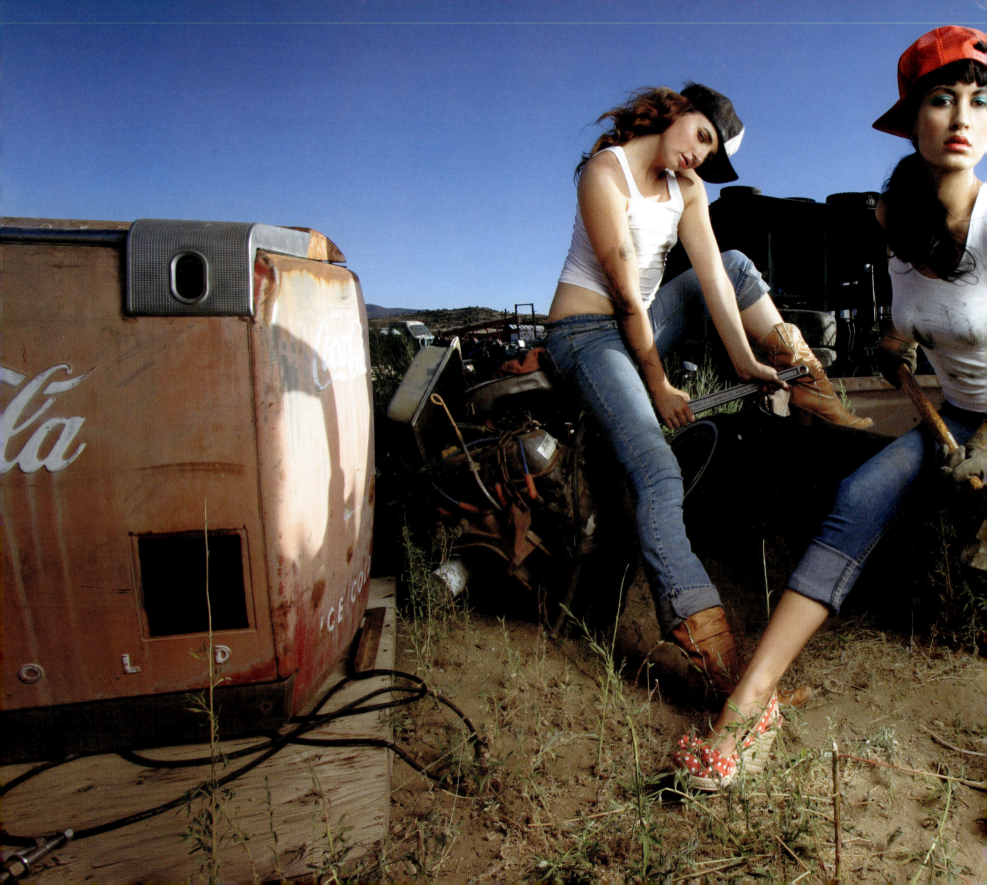

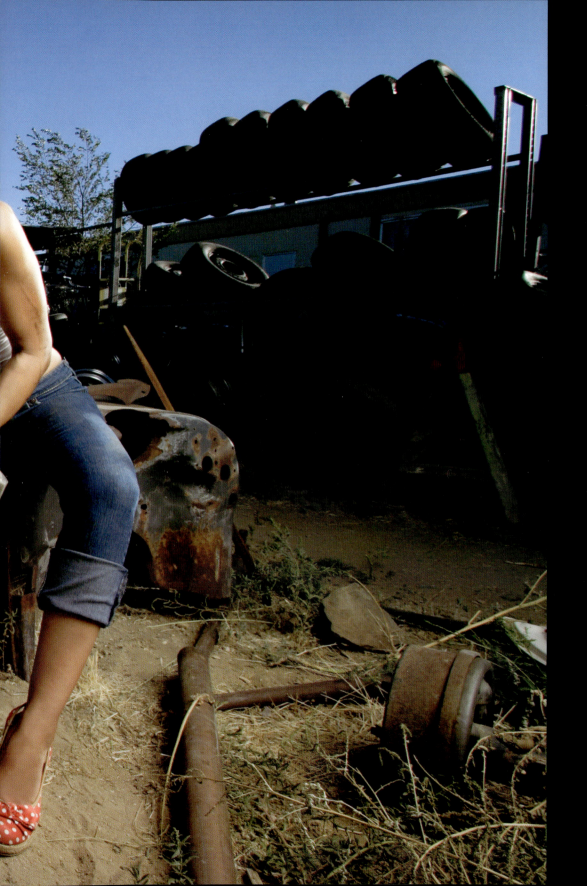

garages and boneyards

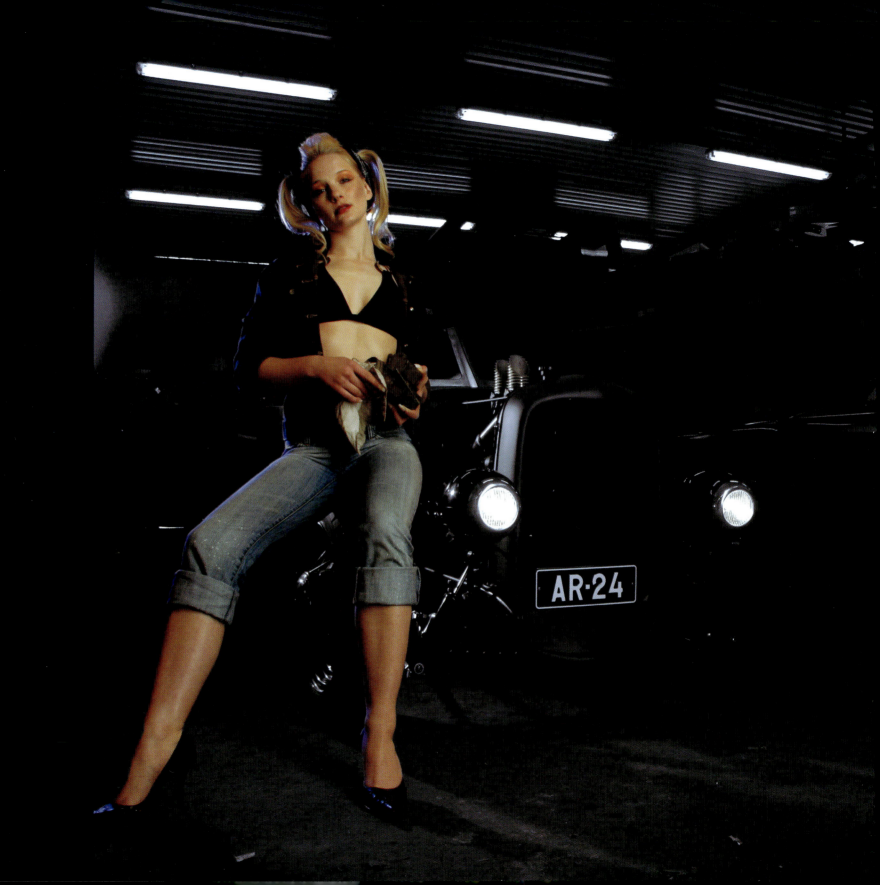

The rule is, while you might see a girl get a lift in a hot rod, you will never see a girl in a junkyard. The two are incompatible. Mutually exclusive.

Junkyards are dirty. They smell. They're gravid with rust, the stench of differential grease, the unique silence of dead iron. And way down South, where me and my junkyards come from, an automobile carcass newly arrived to acres of similar casualties soon enough finds itself interpenetrated by inch-thick blackberry suckers with quarter-inch thorns, a squirrel or two, various species of spider and wasp, and more ticks than an omnibus spending bill has earmarks.

Junkyards have critters and vegetation of all sorts, and guys of course, but girls? It's as if, having been offered free passage out under a flag of truce, they accepted and split.

But there's always an exception . . . .

■ ■ ■

The last and best hot rod I built started out as a 1951 split-windshield half-ton Chevrolet pickup—the one with the narrow bed, flatbed rails, and outboard rear fenders. I found it in a junkyard. It was out front in a whole line of roadworthy vehicles. Two hundred and fifty dollars. Beam axle, Blue Flame six, babbitt bearings cast right on the crank, three on the tree, six-volt electrics. The color was very much the hue of a canned string bean. The tires were tall and narrow, and the hubcaps were small and domed with the Chevrolet name and logo embossed across them in maroon. A vacuum hose from a bib between the carb and the intake manifold ran the windshield wipers, slowly when the RPMs were down, rapidly when they were up.

This truck was amazing. It never failed to start, and under prodigious loads it never staggered. It didn't even leak in the rain. A solid piece of road iron of the sort upon which the American automobile industry built and later forsook its reputation, the truck needed only a few tweaks to make of it a truly great machine.

The truck's first V-8 was a 265, one of the first overhead-valve V-8s in the country. I ordered an adapter kit out of the back of *Hot Rod* magazine, which enabled me to mate the V-8 to the pickup's stock bellhousing. The crane mechanic at the construction company that employed both of us kindly welded two new engine mounts to the forward rails. A pair of Thrush mufflers with a couple of capped pipe nipples welded just in front of them, easily accessible under each rocker panel, completed a mellifluous exhaust system. An extra six-volt battery wired in series with the original to run the 8-track tape deck came in handy, too, for the 265 liked to think in terms of twelve volts not six.

But it became immediately clear that the old six-banger clutch and tranny were not up to the exigencies of a V-8 under the hood and a nineteen-year-old at the wheel. The windshield wipers, on the other hand, now hydroplaned whether it was raining or not, and I had to keep extra wiper blades under the seat.

Being chronically short of cash, I nursed the drivetrain. I commuted twenty miles a day to and from work, and it was utterly reliable. Even the heater worked. Often, in a conversion like this, windshield wipers, heaters, turn signals, and parking lamps are early casualties. But I had the fortune to do much of the work in the crane shop, where hoses, clamps, tempered drill bits, and even a floor lift were readily available. I was equally fortunate in the crane mechanic, who had probably built forty racecars and whiskey runners before I finished kicking the slats out of my crib.

Soon enough, however, it came time to step up to a 327.

Now, Detroit produced all kinds of engines, many of them rightfully famous. The flathead Ford, America's first V-8, comes to mind, as does the three-deuce Pontiac 389, Chevy's porcupine-valve 396, Ford's dual-overhead-cam 427, the old Lincoln 460, and, of course, Chrysler's storied Hemi. But in the 327, Chevrolet produced a masterpiece. And throughout the 1960s and 1970s, 327s could readily be had in junkyards across the nation.

I found mine in a junkyard on the west side of Monroe, North Carolina, not far from the railroad tracks. "Sho 'nuf," allowed the tobacco-chewing man behind the desk in the unpainted shack that tilted next to the yard entrance. "There's a 327 in that Suburban." He swiveled his chair and pointed out the backdoor, leaned forward, and spat through same. "Take a hunnert dollars for her."

I followed his squint along the slope of wrecks up to the corner of the yard, and there, just like he said, sat what was left of a Chevrolet Suburban, late-'60s vintage. It looked like somebody had driven a train through the passenger door.

"Nawp," the man behind the desk said. "Her final hand wuz dealt by a chicken truck." He spat again. Not all of the juice clearing his whiskers, he plucked a pink mechanic's rag from among the papers and fan belts and radiator hoses and a half-eaten nickel package of saltine crackers on his desk and wiped his face. "You gotta truck?"

"Fifty-two Chevy." I pointed toward the front door. "I'm gonna drop that mill right into it," I added proudly.

The owner evinced no interest whatsoever in the engine's future. "You got cash, we'll skip the tax."

I frowned. "It'll run?"

"She was runnin' when the truck hit her," the man said, "and there warn't no damage from the firewall forwards."

A hundred dollars for a functioning 327 was a good deal, all right. But I felt it incumbent not to make a deal for something about which I knew next to nothing. "Which 327 is it?"

"It'll be the two-fifty," the man said right away, referring to the rated horsepower.

"The two-barrel," I responded, a little disappointed.

"That's your grandmother's car," the owner confirmed.

Two hundred and fifty horsepower seemed a mite puny back then, though it was more ponies than the 265 could muster, and a mere four-barrel carburetor over an adapter plate would allow that same 327 to creep up on 275 horsepower; polished and ported with a camshaft it would easily crest 300; a proper intake manifold and headers with a thorough balancing job, and you were burning rubber from second to third—with a righteous clutch and transmission, of course. And you didn't have to stop there. The mill's genetics were unquestionable, and the price was right.

"Done," I said. I handed my hard-earned money over the desk. The man fanned the twenties in one hand, saw there were five of them, folded them double, and kicked the plank wall adjacent the back-door. "James! Run up yonder and git the motor out that Chevrolet station wagon. Leave the transmission on the ground. Jist the motor." The owner turned to me. "You got two foot of chain?" I had twenty feet, with a hook at each end. "Go git it." I went and got it. The owner handed the pile out the door to James and told him, "Drap it in that itty-sompin' pickup out front. And don't be gittin' lost, neither. This boy here's in a hurry to be hot roddin'. After yer done," he tucked one

of the twenties into the bib of James' coveralls and turned his voice sweet, "take this hyar across the road and git us a pint."

James' eyes lit up and he abstracted himself out the door with payday alacrity.

After a moment, an unmuffled engine rumbled to life out back and we watched a pickup truck with a homemade derrick in the bed and no window glass or license plate maneuver up a winding, muddy slope toward the Suburban, a pair of oxyacetylene tanks rattling against the back of the cab. Once there, James backed up the truck to the front bumper of the wreck. In a trice he removed the hood and applied bolt cutters to every wire, hose, and linkage that had connected the engine to anything else. Then he looped one end o my chain under one of the ram's horn exhaust manifolds, draped i over the derrick's hook, and looped it again under the opposite ram's horn and knotted it. Once he'd taken up the slack, he fired up the torch and made short work of the engine mounts, as well as the exhaust pipes. Finally, he writhed up under the car and spun off the nuts o the tranny's universal joint. Soon enough, voilà, one 327 V-8 dangled off his hook.

Back in the shack, having issued me a greasy receipt, the owner tore the lid off a can of Vienna sausages. As he retrieved the first one the most difficult one to remove from the can, I wandered out the backdoor and watched as James pulled the wrecker forward, dropped the engine to the mud, and spun the bolts off the starter and bell housing with an air wrench.

Not five minutes later, the springs under the bed of my pickup were accommodating the weight of my brand-new used 327. Dropping the rest of my chain into the bed with it, James drove the wrecker across the paved road and disappeared up the rutted track that led to a pool hall.

Immediately, I saw that the owner of the junkyard had let both o us in for a surprise. In the process of his manipulations, James had o necessity removed the engine's air filter, exposing not the anticipated two-barrel carb atop the quotidian mill used to propel groceries to home and family to church, but a twin-float four-barrel, indubitabl a stock item. There was only one configuration of the Chevy 327 tha came from the factory with that puppy installed.

I didn't have to look twice. I jumped in the cab and reached for the switch.

"Goddammit," the owner roared from the front door of the shack the can of sausages in one hand and the pink mechanic's rag in the other. "That sonofabitch is worth two hunnert and fitty dollars!"

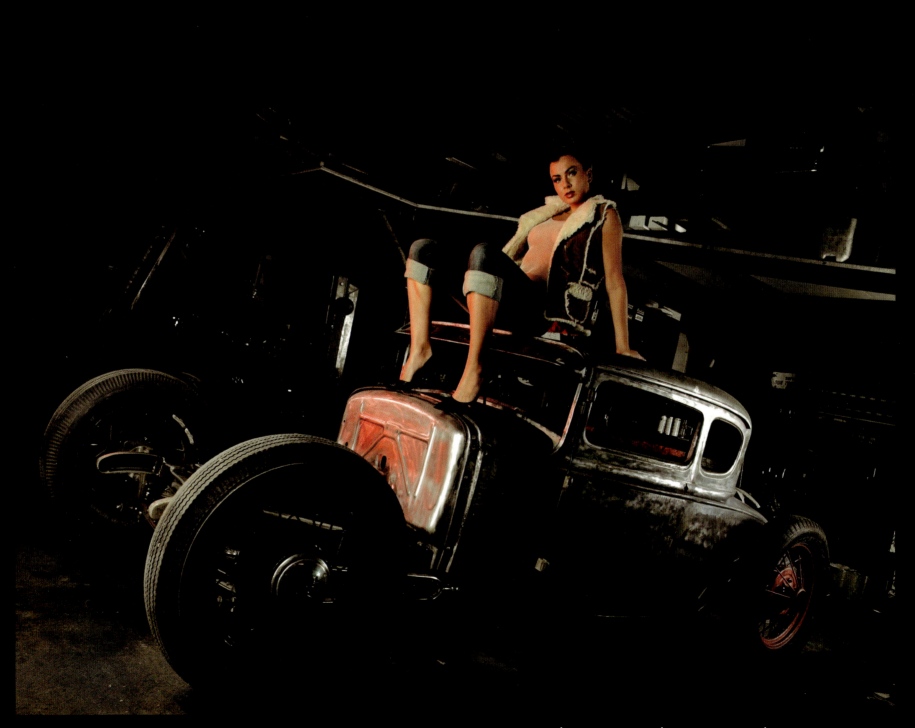

NIINA | 1930 Ford Model A | Owner: Anssi Tarna | Location: Helsinki, Finland

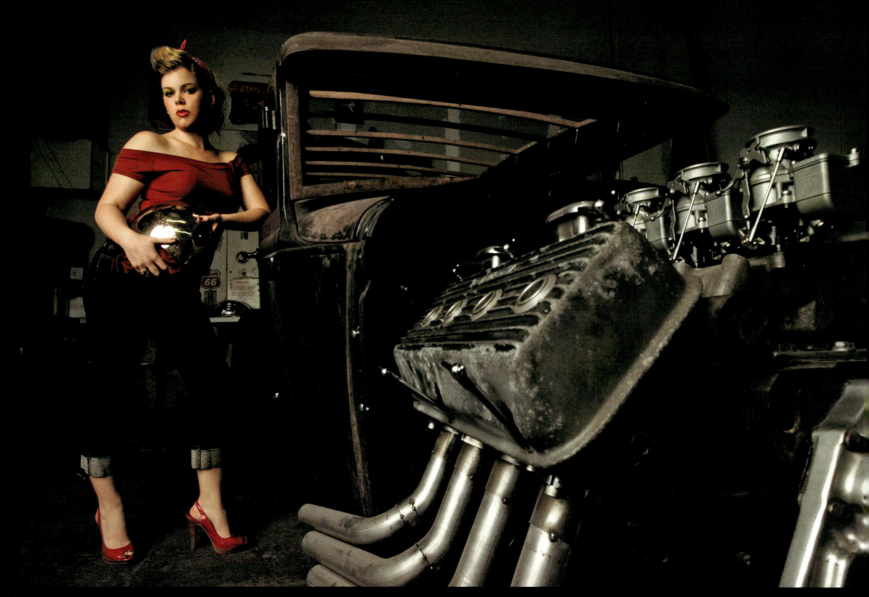

DANAE | 1931 Ford Sedan, Ted Gotelli Hemi with M/T heads | Owner: Eric Jones | Location: Kid Built, Richmond, California

The 265 caught on the first round, as I had tuned it to do. I pulled it into first and showed my receipt out the window.

"Sonofabitch," was all the owner said. It was all he could say. "Bought and paid fer. The damn thing is yourn."

He sounded like one of those people who blame meter maids for tickets. "Some little old lady was fooling a lot of people," I suggested consolingly.

"And I'm at the ass-end of the line," the owner admitted morosely.

"Well, it's in the back of your truck now."

"And it's soon be in the front end," I reminded him.

He gestured with the can of sausage. "Git on down the road, then, so I can be shed of the sight of her. Dogged if you ain't put one over on me, son," he added ruefully.

"See you all real soon," I lied, and eased the clutch.

The owner watched me pull onto the paved highway. As soon as I got out of sight of the junkyard, I eased over and tied down the load. I wasn't about to lose that engine at that point.

So there you have it—a short rundown of the rule, pretty much.

Now for the exception.

■ ■ ■

The 327 dropped into the truck like a cartridge into a breach.

Within a few months and a few paychecks, I had a pair of fifteen-inch Mickey Thompson magnesium wheels out back with some seriously fat tires mounted on them. Up front were the stock rims, but they sported a pair of steel-belted radials—unusual for the time. In order for the rear wheelwells to accommodate the tires, I installed a late-'50s Mercury rearend—another trip to another junkyard.

Up front, with the distributor advanced by some twelve degrees, my 300-horsepower 327 roared to life halfway through its first revolution. Little did they know the resulting compression was such that if the battery was the least bit weak, the thing wouldn't turn over at all.

The ever-increasing power of the V-8 wreaked havoc on clutches and transmissions. They just weren't up to the task, and I burned up two or three each. I'd about cleaned out the county's junkyards of early-'50s three-speed truck trannies.

A Corvette or, better, a 409 four-speed was, of course, the solution. But such transmissions translated into serious money, which I didn't have. I couldn't go back to the junkyard in Monroe. For sure, the owner would try to make up for his loss on the 327. So I flayed the brush for alternatives, of which there were plenty. We're talking the rural South—every town had a junkyard, every county had several little towns, and North Carolina has 100 counties.

One Saturday afternoon me and the '52 took a dirt road we'd never traveled before. It went south and then east, skirting along the South Carolina border toward Fayetteville, home of the 101st Airborne, or Fayette-Nam, as we called it in those years.

That road never did turn back into asphalt. We trundled along it for an hour or more, trailing a plume of red dust. Despite the traction bars I'd recently installed, or perhaps because of them, the truck was fun to handle on that surface. Second gear kept things wound just tight enough to break traction at the slightest excuse.

We dipped down into creek bottoms and over little one-way bridges, crowned rises between pastures lightly populated by Black Angus, and skirted a quarry on a ridge from which one could see that nothing but willows, white oaks, pastures, and kudzu stretched for miles in any direction.

And then we found it. At an intersection where the dirt road crossed another stood a gas station, a store, and a vast junkyard. Vast and . . . tidy.

Neatly, I brought the truck to a stop, throwing only a little gravel against the outside wall of the office. As the dust swirled around the cab, I could see that this place was different. The wrecker was painted yellow and purple, it got washed often, and a lei hung from the cab's rearview mirror. Everything in its bed was in its place and clean. The oxyacetylene tanks were their natural colors—green and tan—and the hoses were neatly coiled. The gas-powered compressor looked brand new, although, judging by its design, it clearly wasn't. Shovels and pinch bars, a chainsaw, and miscellaneous other tools were clean and neatly arrayed in a rack. A galvanized bucket full of case-hardened chain had been painted pink.

Under each of the two windows facing the road and flanking the office door hung a flower box—in one bloomed purple and yellow pansies, and in the other flowered daffodils and pink tulips. A yellow watering can with daisies painted on it sat atop the stoop leading into the office. The dog that got up to greet me did not snarl, but wagged its tail. He wasn't mangy, either, or even dirty. As I stepped into the office and brushed his back, my hand encountered no oil-soaked mat of fur, nor a single swollen tick.

And the owner?

The owner was a lithe blonde, precisely my age, with grey eyes. She wore a pair of freshly laundered overalls, striped white and blue, a tank top underneath—modest enough, to be sure, but different she was. Different entirely from the last vendor I described in detail.

And how did I know that this woman was my own age?

Because I'd met her before.

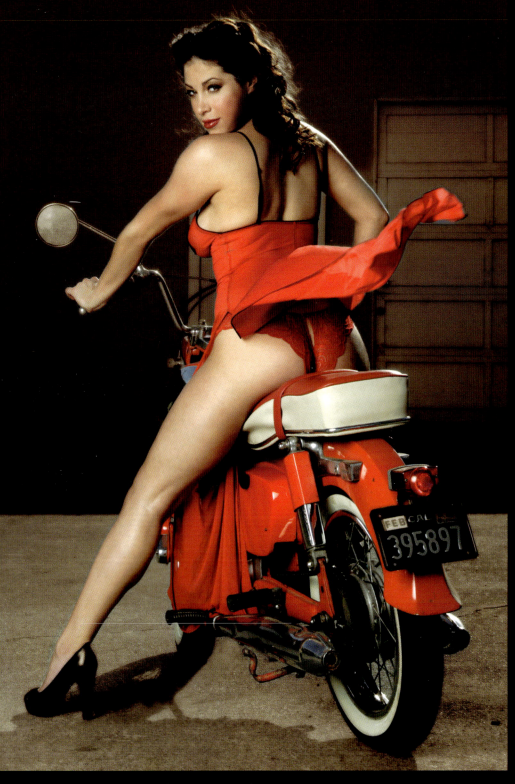

"Belinda?"

"Jim?"

"Belinda Cox—is that you?"

"I might ask you the same question!" Belinda smiled warmly. She immediately pulled a Cheerwine out of a cooler humming in the corner of the office, right behind a bench seat, baby blue with white piping, extracted, it looked like, from somebody's baby blue Ford Bronco. I noticed several cans of PBR, too, cooling among the soft drinks.

"Well, thank you," I said, taking a mighty swallow. "It's hot and that's for sure."

Well, indeed, for only two or three mighty swallows will stand in for decent conversation, and after an awkward silence, I blurted the question: "What are you doing, uh, here?"

"Here?"

"In a, er, junkyard."

"Why, this is my daddy's junkyard. I grew up in it."

"Oh. And where is your daddy?"

"In the store yonder, playing checkers. Or he's asleep on the porch swing off to one side, maybe."

"Oh."

"So."

"So. . . ."

I learned that she had dropped out of the University of North Carolina, where I had met her, to come home and attend her mother's last illness. That had been a year ago. She planned to return to college the next fall, which would make for a nearly two-year lapse in her education.

"Civil engineering, was it?"

"Very good," she said. "You have an excellent memory."

"Well, how could I forget the only woman in Numerical Analysis? Let alone the prettiest."

Right there, my voice hung up. Just stopped. After an embarrassing and extended pause, my voice made none of the sounds that pass for coherent language.

When Belinda's laughter had subsided, she asked, "Tell me, what are you doing here?"

At last—something easy to talk about! "I need a transmission," I began. "And not any transmission. See that short out there?"

"No," she said, heading for the door for a look. "But I heard it."

Did this girl know what to say, or what?

"A 327," she declared, pausing with one hand on the door frame, "in that heap?"

"A 327," I confirmed. "And that's my heap."

Well," she pronounced with unrestrained enthusiasm, "cool!"

Boy, did I get a laugh out of that. I might never have felt so good in my life. But it got better.

"Take me for a ride?" she said.

I could hardly believe my ears. "What about the yard?"

She laughed outright. "Oh, Shelby there," she said, indicating the dog, "will keep an eye on things while we're gone."

But the minute I opened the passenger door, Shelby hopped up on the seat. Shelby may or may not have known a cool ride when he saw it, but every dog in the world knows what a pickup truck is for.

We were a long way out in the country. Belinda didn't even close the door of the office, let alone draw closed the gate to the yard. "When we get back," she assured me, "all that junk will still be here. Besides, Daddy's right across the road."

While entirely complimentary about the sound and look and feel of the ride, and equally skeptical about the way it looked, Belinda saw immediately that I was babying the transmission, that the synchronizer ring was gone from first and reverse, and that the clutch was slipping.

"So," I said, as we bounced along the fourth or fifth dirt track she'd directed us down, "what happened to, uh—I forget his name. Your boyfriend."

"Fiancé," she corrected. "His name was Frank Fontayne. Still is, I reckon. He couldn't stand the separation and got himself another girl. Plus, Daddy never did like him. Probably why I did like him, at first, come to analyze me."

I wasn't about to do any analyzing. I indicated the dog. "And Shelby?"

"The two times Frank came here, once to see me, and again to attend Momma's funeral, Shelby just watched him."

"Good boy," I said.

Shelby, who sat between us on the seat, closed his eyes and rolled his head under my hand.

"Hey," Belinda said. "He was my fiancé. And that's my dog."

"Family is a big deal," I observed sententiously. "And dogs know everything. Uh . . . 'was'?"

"Past tense."

"Miss him?"

"No," she said matter-of-factly. "So you need a transmission."

"I need a transmission."

"Why not go for a four-speed?"

"Too much money."

"You need a clutch, too."

"More money."

"Relined the brakes lately?"

I shook my head.

"How fast will this heap go?"

The stock speedometer ran off a gear in the tail shaft of the stock transmission. The instantaneous windup of the 327, along with its many RPMs, had spun it to flinders long since. "Faster than I want to go."

"What's the differential ratio?"

I replied instantly, a thrill running up my spine, "Three-point-seven to one."

"And the tire size?"

I told her.

"A hundred and ten, anyway," she speculated.

"That's right when I chicken out," I agreed. "Besides, all the fun is in the getting there. There's not too many places where you can do a hundred miles an hour, get away with it, and be safe, too."

"Not to mention wore-out brakes and a beam axle."

"True story. But I got Load-Levelers all the way around."

"Excellent. Let's go back."

"Already?"

"I want to show you something."

When I put that Mercury rear end out back, it had been hell to reinstall the handbrake. But that day it all became worth it. I pumped the brake pedal twice, depressed the clutch, cranked the wheel all the way to the left, and pulled the handbrake. The truck made a perfect bootlegger's turn, coming to a stop facing the direction from which it had been traveling, with the engine still running. It didn't hurt that we were on a sand roadbed.

■ ■ ■

Belinda opened the door of an ancient tobacco house way in the back of the junkyard. A kerosene lantern and a box of kitchen matches were inside. As Belinda trimmed the wick, I could see that the shed contained nothing but transmissions and differentials, row upon row of them, in wood racks, stacked six and eight feet off the floor. Each was labeled. And each was pretty clean, too, more or less, though the stench of lube was nearly as overpowering as the reek of sloughed snakeskin. "It's in here somewhere." She slid a milk crate in front of a stack of trannies and stood atop it. "Aha. Come up here and look at this." There was barely enough room for the two of us. She stood on tiptoe, holding my shoulder with one hand and pointing to the topmost transmission with the other. "That's a 1959 Chevrolet three-speed," she told me. "It'll handle your 327, and it's got one very special feature."

"What's that?"

"Overdrive."

"What?"

"Point eight to one. They only made it that one year."

I had never heard of such a thing. But, if true, it meant that this obscure transmission was effectively a four-speed. "It must be incredibly rare," I observed.

"I've only seen the one," Belinda agreed. "Daddy says that after the four-speed came in, nobody wanted them."

I touched one of the shifter dogs on the side of the housing. "How much do you want for it?"

"Daddy told me it should be worth sixty dollars." Belinda smiled. "But for you? Forty dollars and a kiss."

Her eyes weren't six inches from my own. "What-what," I stammered, "what if the dog bites me?"

Shelby stood on the stoop and rolled his eyes up at us, not unlike an old man peering over his bifocals. Belinda put her arms around me, and I certainly must have blushed as red as the lantern base. "Well Shelby," she asked the dog, "What about it?"

Shelby wagged his tail tentatively.

■ ■ ■

The transmission fit fine. I had to find a certain Pontiac driveshaft to cope with its length, for the tranny's tail shaft was unusually long to accommodate the overdrive. While I was at it, I found a 409 clutch and bellhousing, so the hot rodding of universal joints necessary to marry Chevy to Pontiac to Mercury was worth the trouble. Once accomplished, my drivetrain problems were over.

Belinda and I saw each other on and off for six or seven months. I readily let her drive the truck, and she readily accepted the opportunity. But what she really wanted to do was go back to school. When the University of Colorado offered her a scholarship, she headed west for Boulder and we never saw each other again.

Shelby wound up living with me.

Every time I flicked that electric overdrive switch, the 327 dropped from, say, 3,500 to 2,800 RPMs with no corresponding drop in speed, as if spontaneously, mysteriously, magically inventing new room to accelerate. And with no sign of the whole world running out of highway any time soon, I always thought of Belinda.

And often Shelby, who always was perched on the passenger seat, looking out the window, would notice the change in sound, as the tranny dropped into overdrive. He'd glance over his shoulder, down toward the bootless hole in the floorboard, cut out for the floor shifter, and then he'd look up at me.

I never saw another woman in a junkyard.

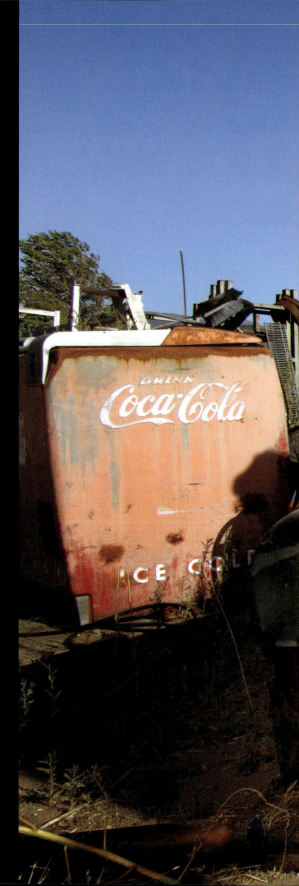

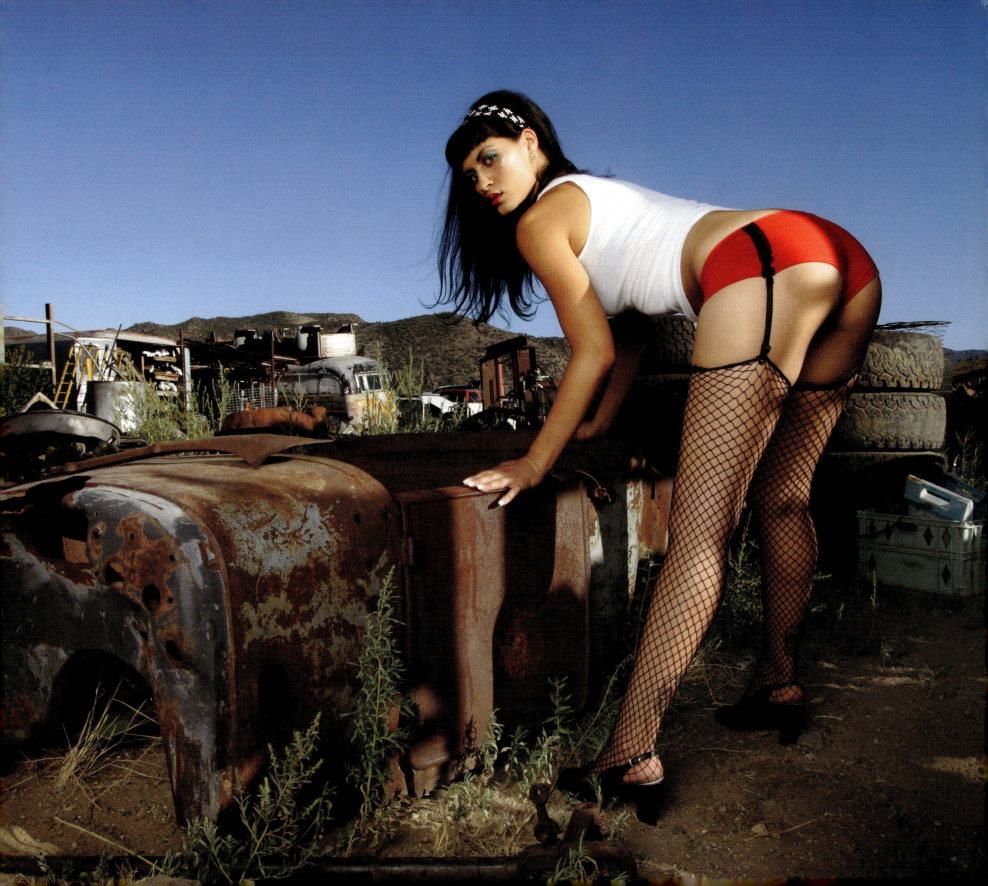

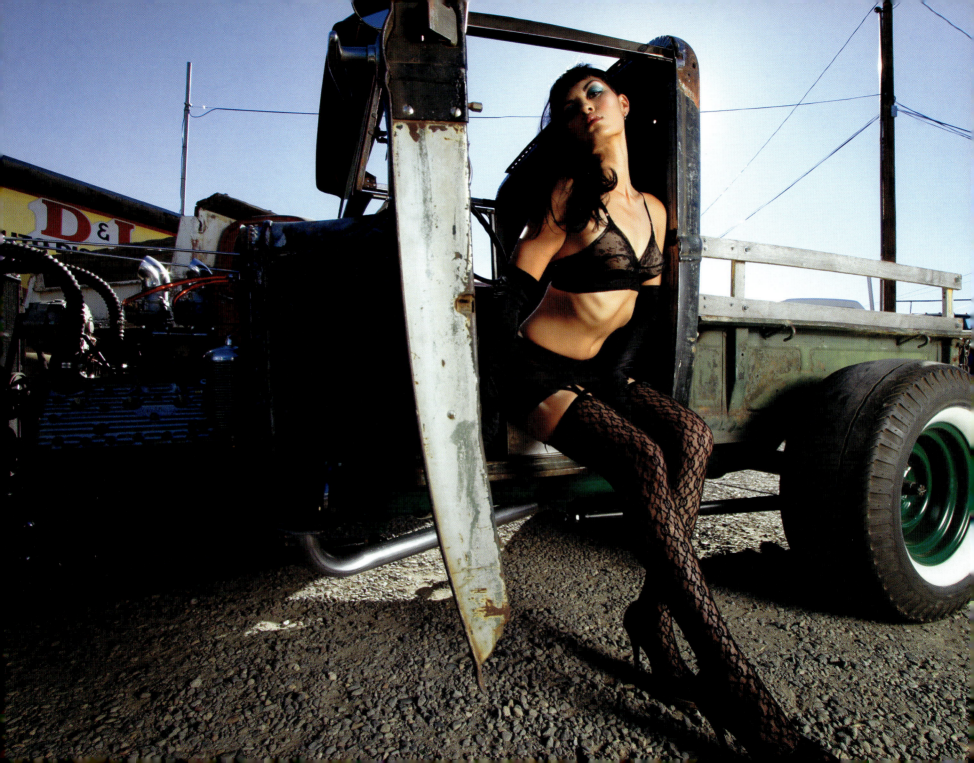

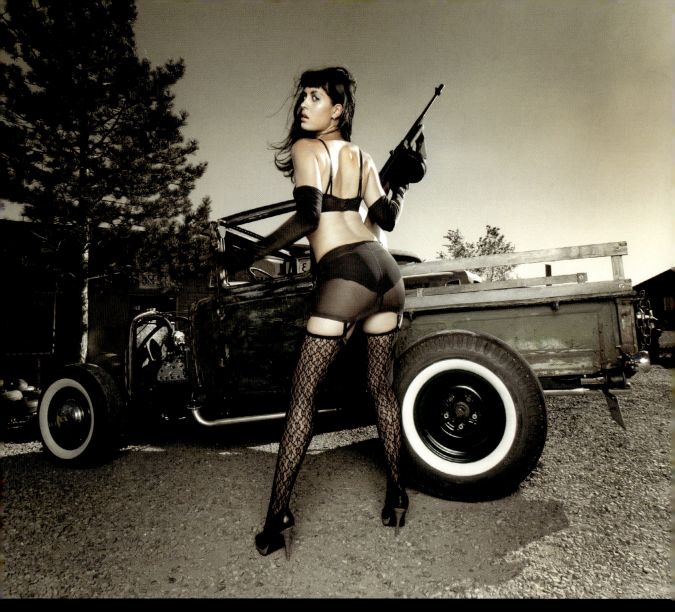

SARAH   Model A Ford Pickup with Flathead   Owner: Richard   Location: Dick's Auto Sales and Rebuilding, Mound House, Nevada

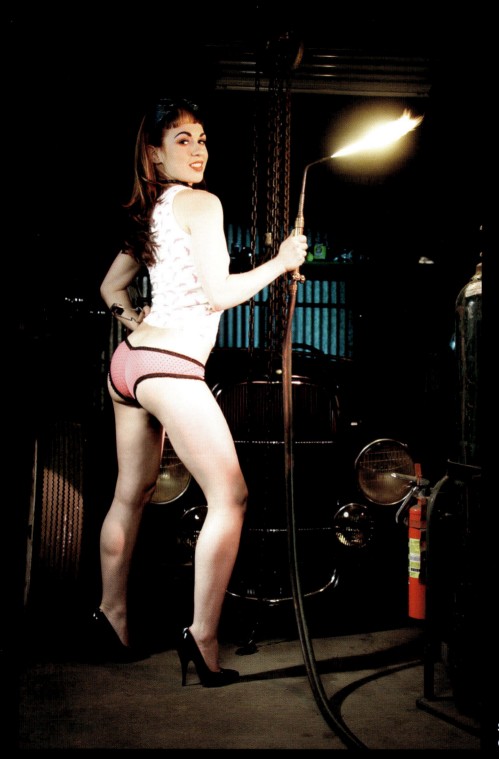

SASHA | 1927 Model T Ford with 1956 303 Oldsmobile Rocket 88
Owner: Matt Seret | Location: Vallejo, California

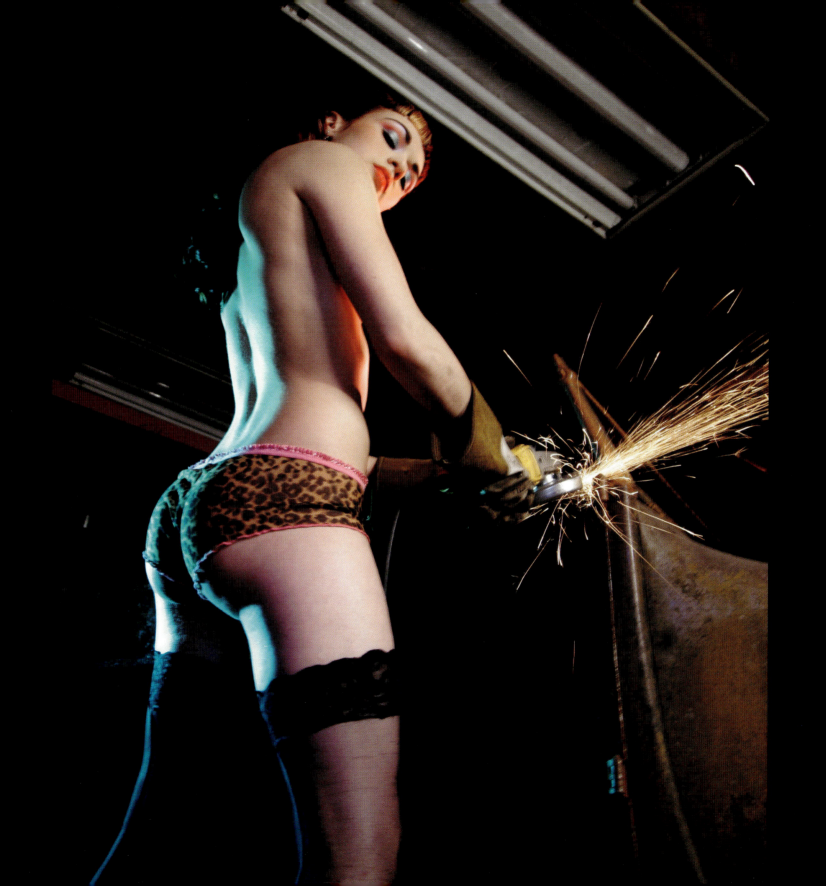

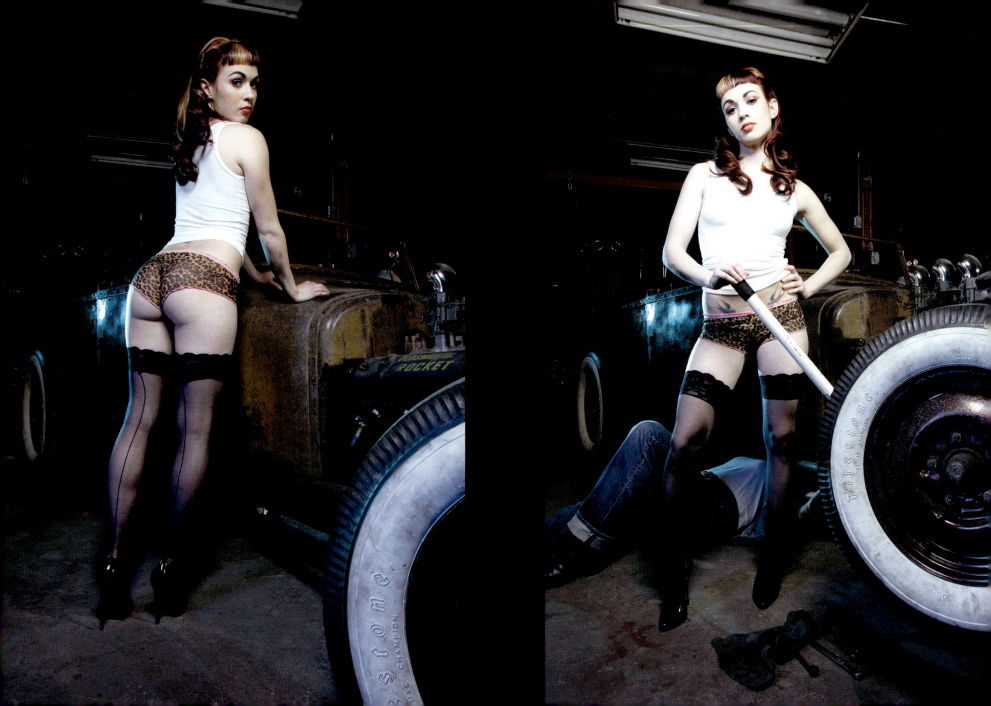

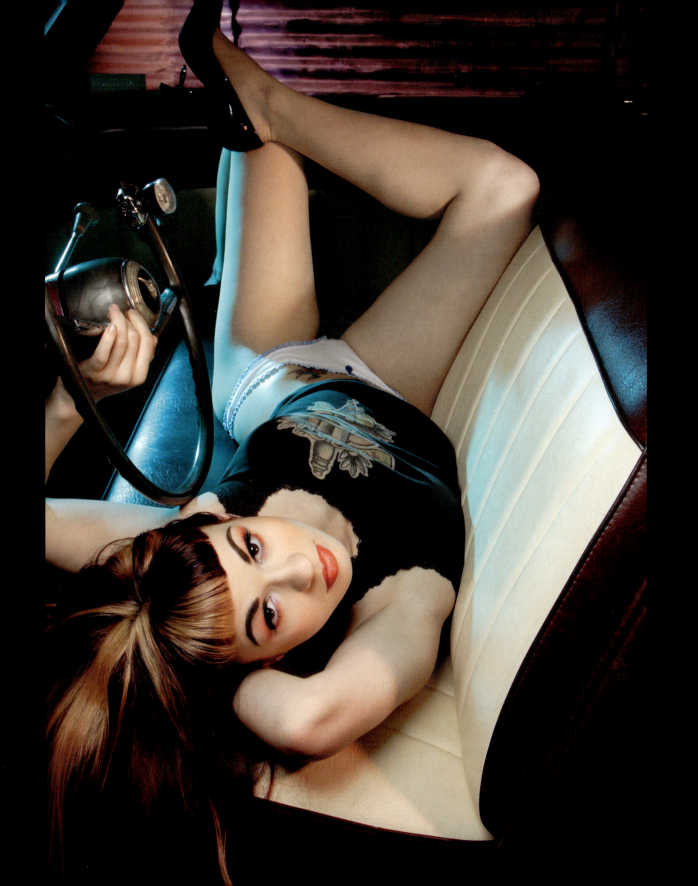

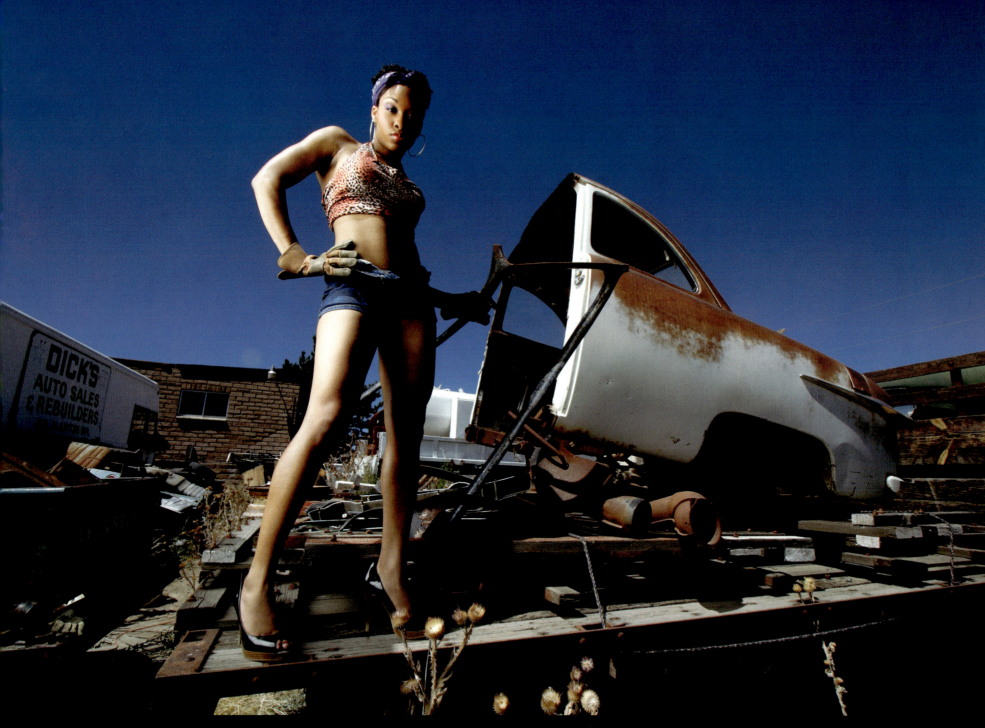

1950 Ford   Location: Dick's Auto Sales and Rebuilding, Mound House, Nevada

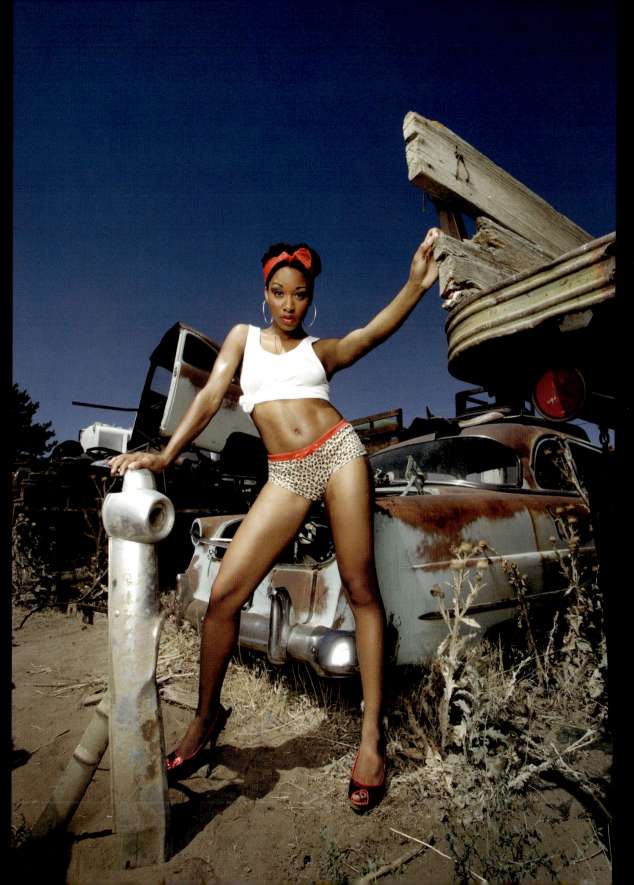

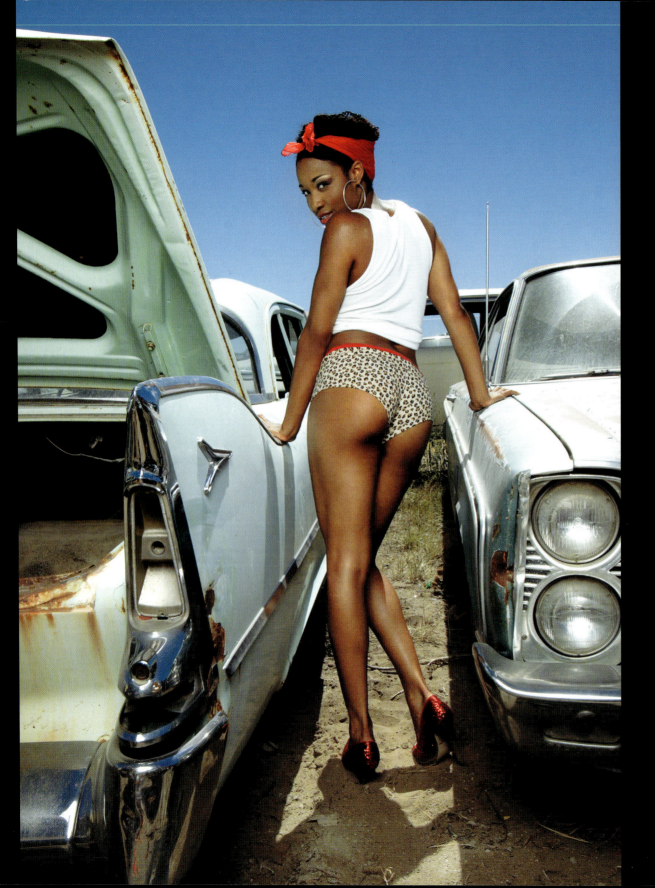
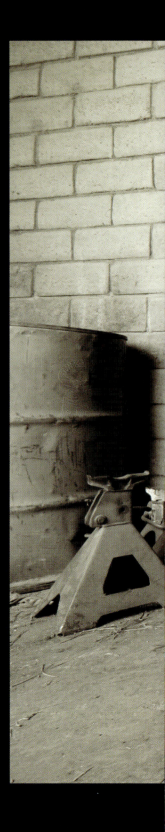

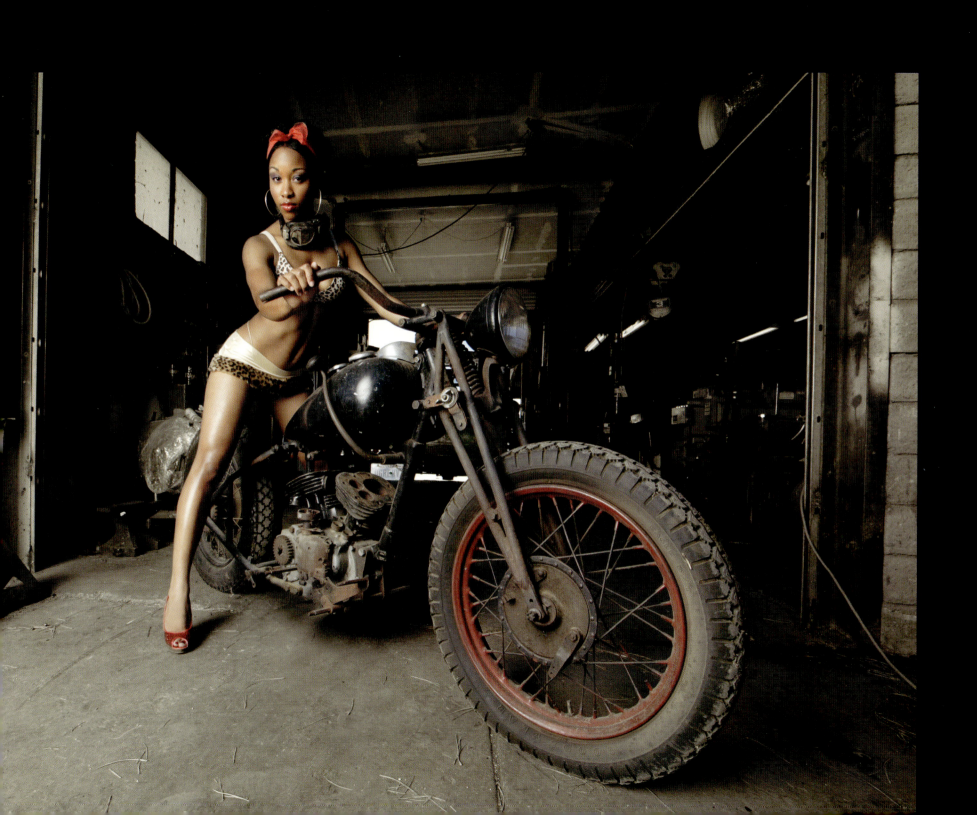

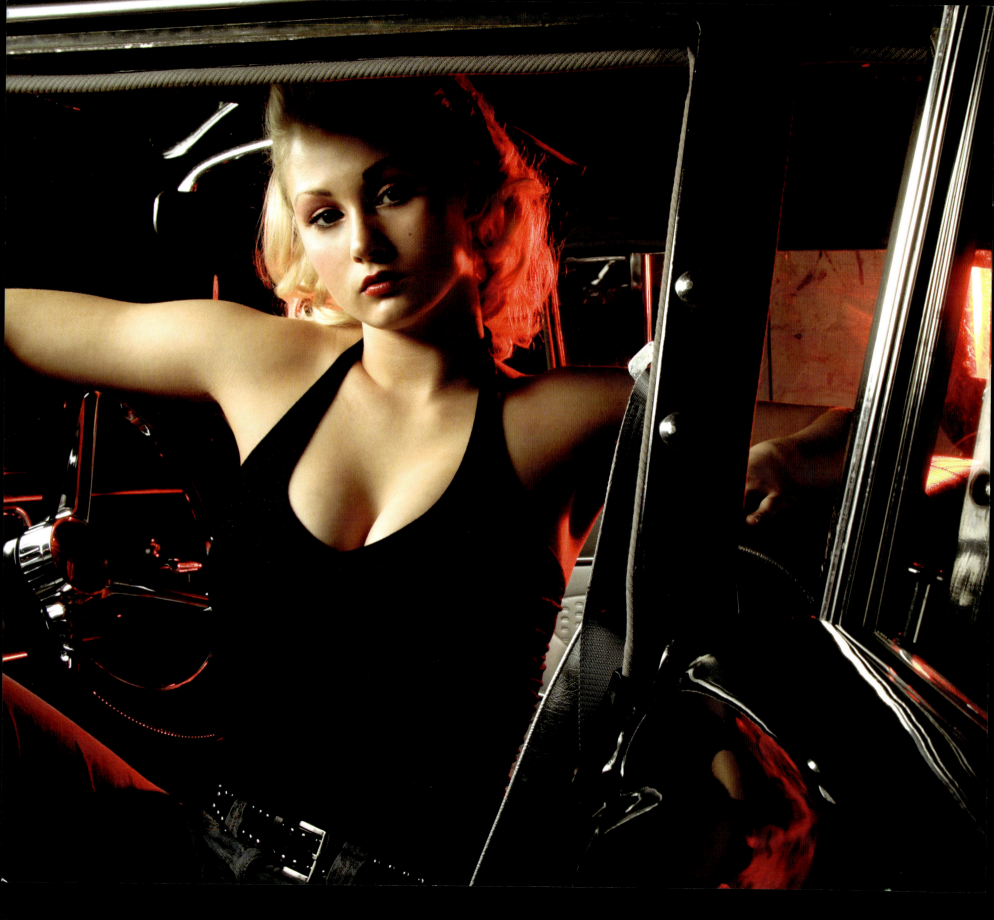

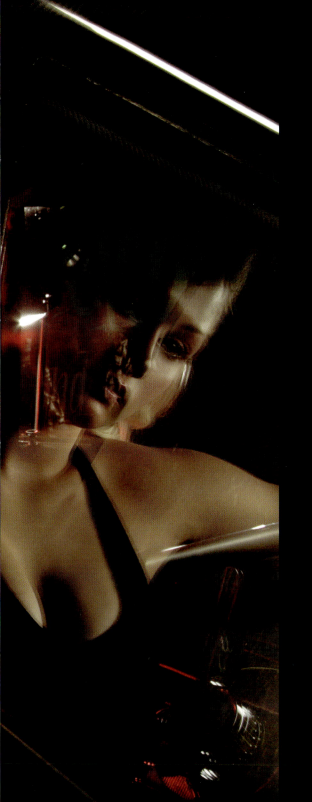
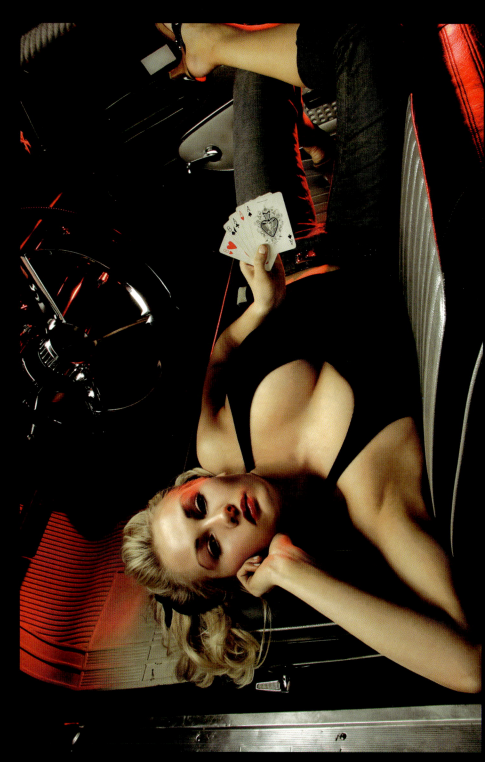

HELI | Club: Tomahawk Town | Location: Helsinki, Finland

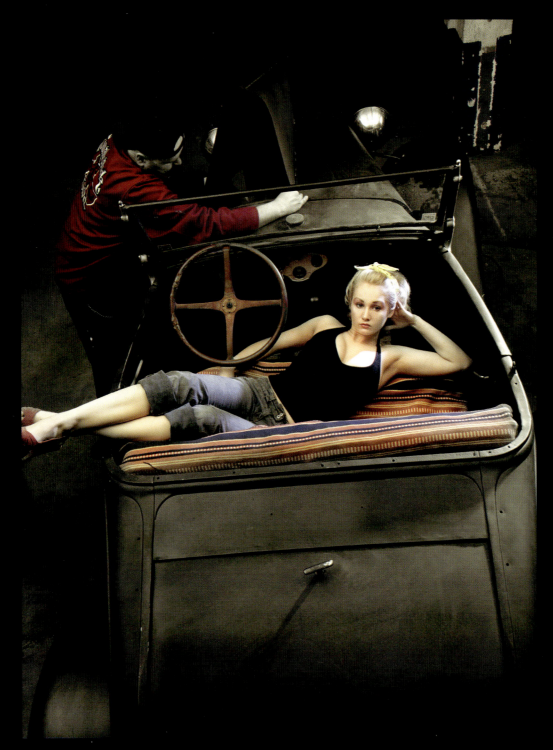

HELI | 1930 Ford Model A | Owner: Unu Vinhava | Club: Tomahawk Town | Location: Helsinki, Finland

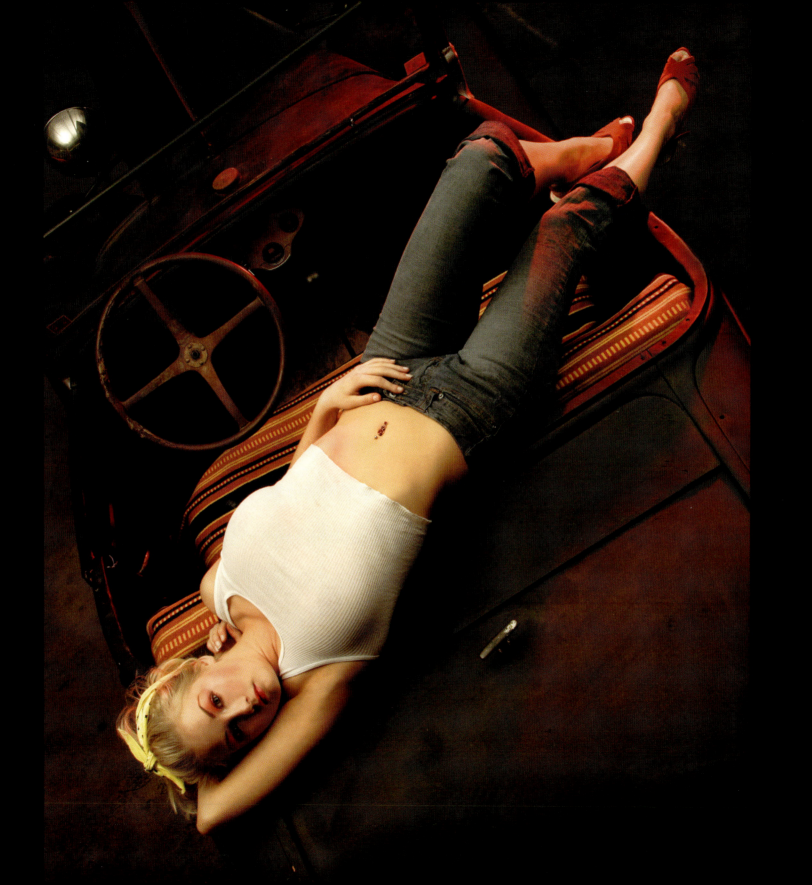

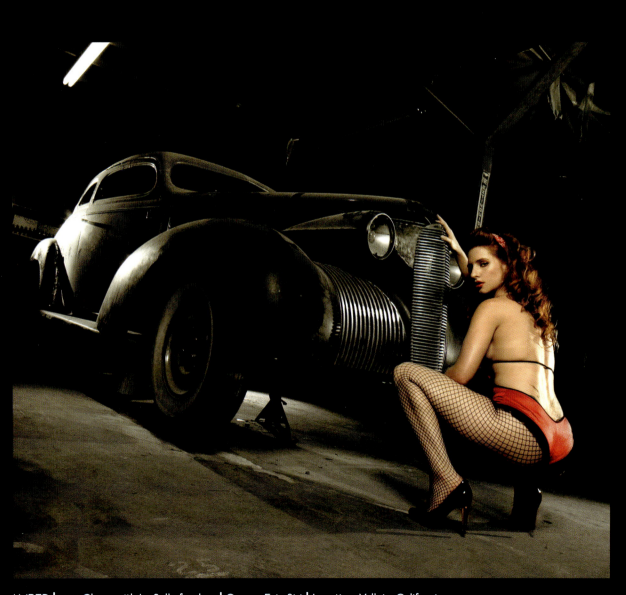

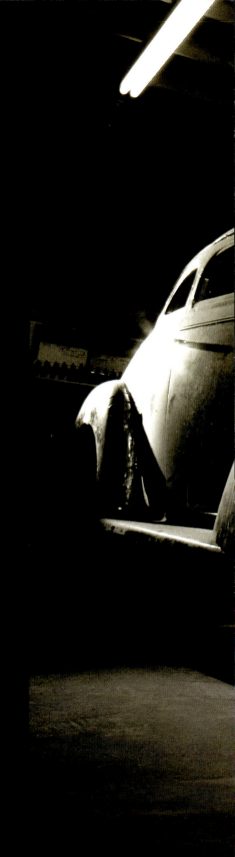

AMBER | 1939 Chevy with La Salle fenders | Owner: Ezio Siri | Location: Vallejo, California

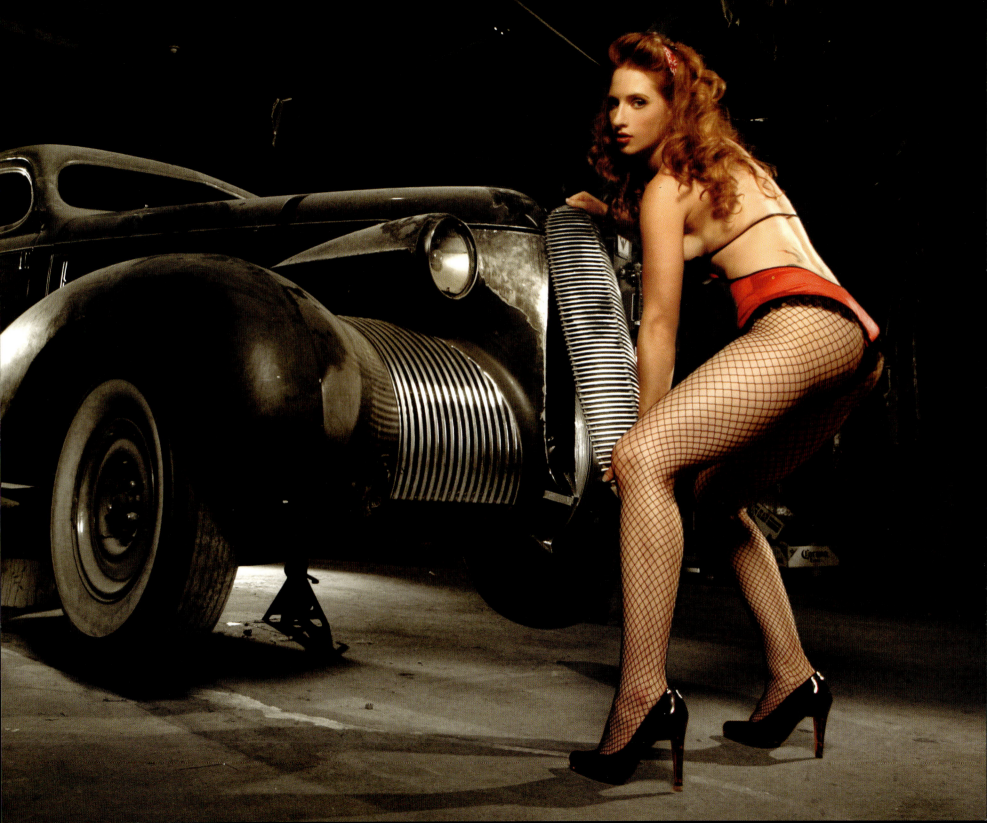

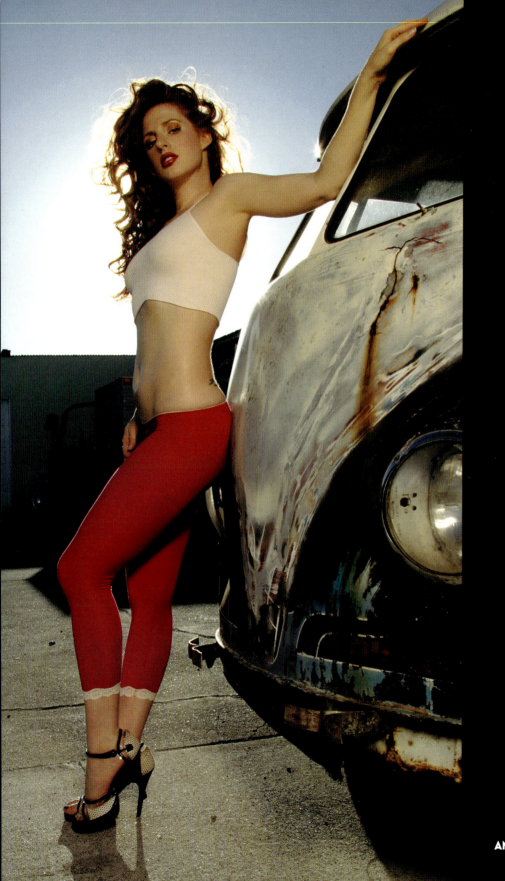

AMBER | 1962 VW Bus | Owner: Ezio Siri | Location: Vallejo, California

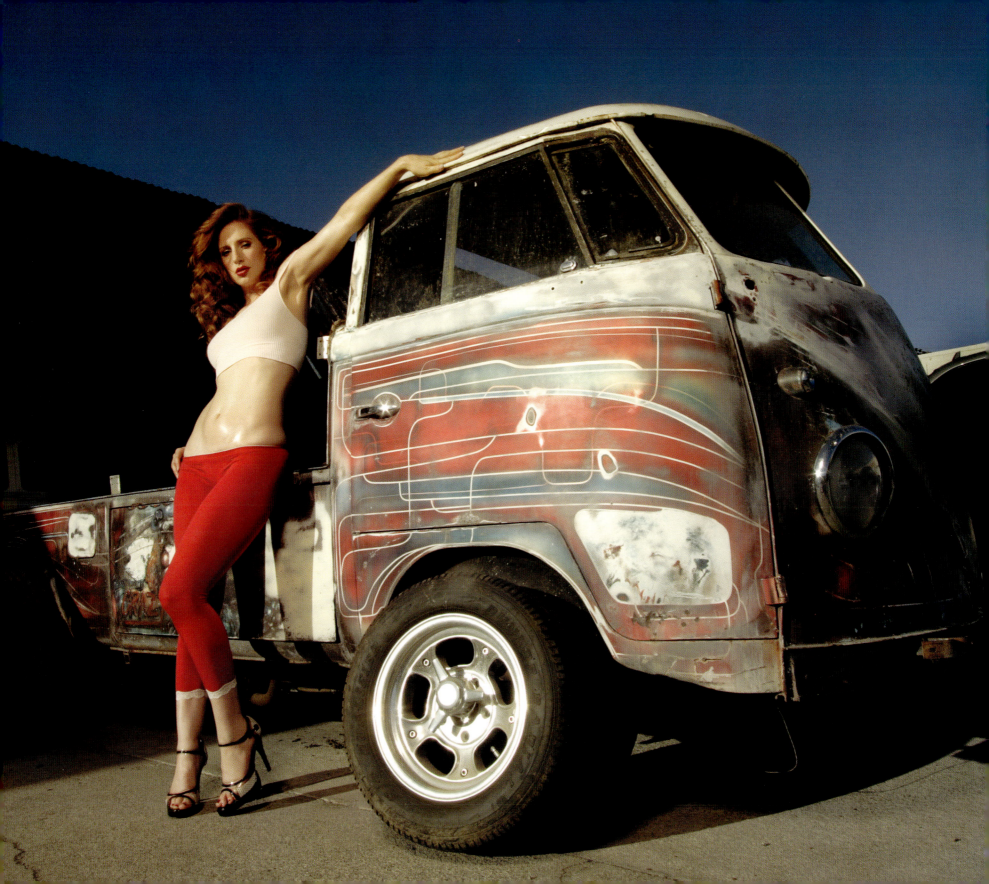

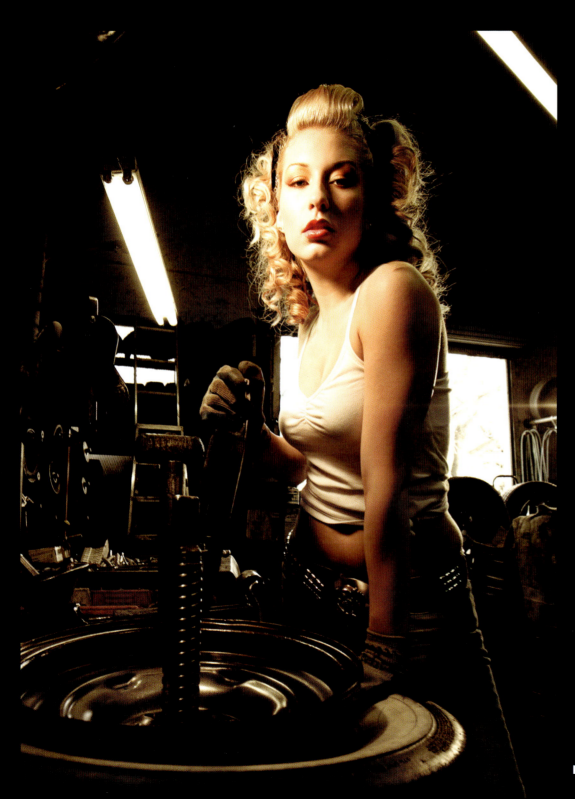

HALEY | Location: The Used Tire Shop, Vacaville, California

38

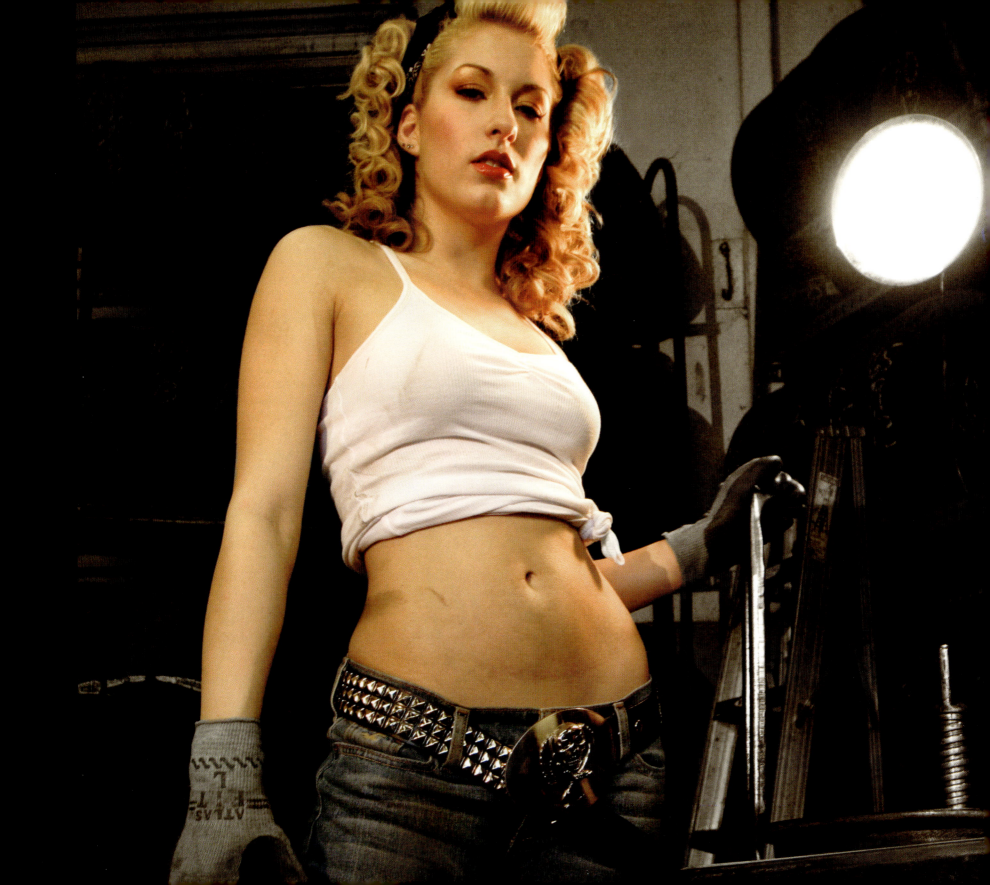

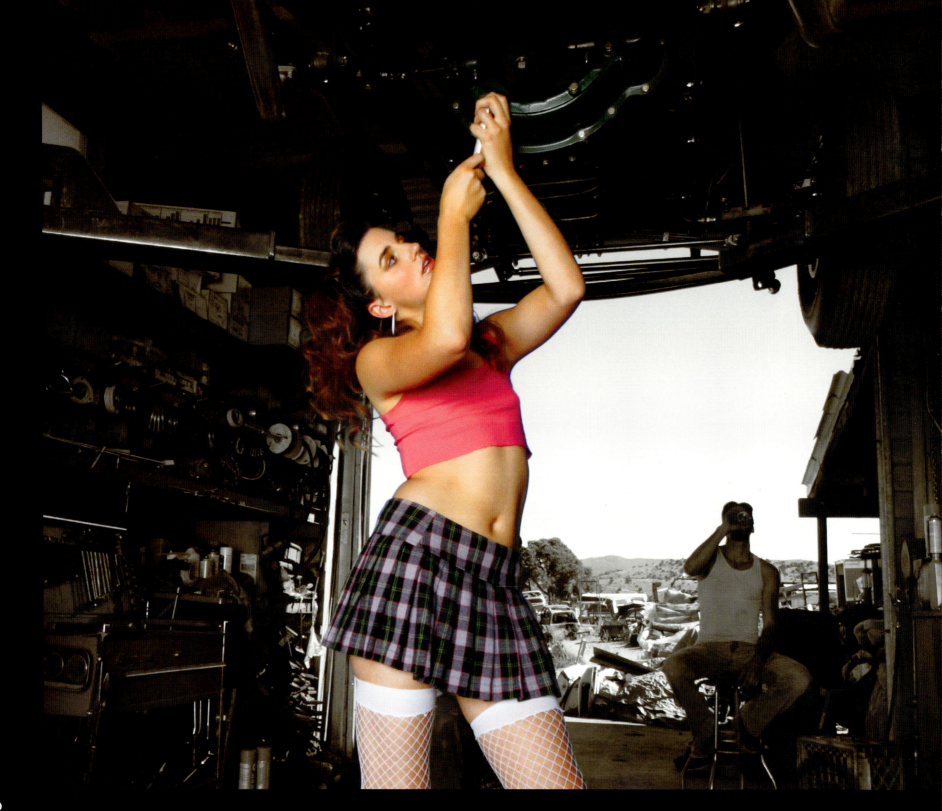

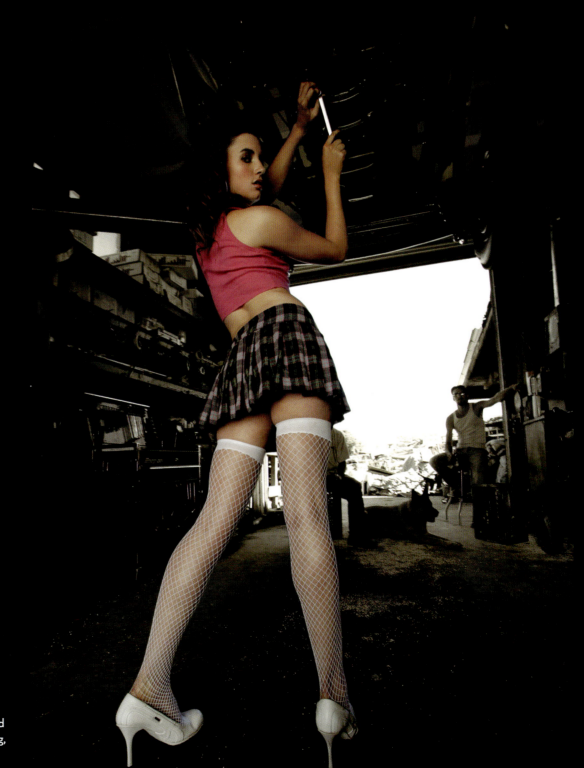

NICKI | Model A Ford Pickup with Flathead
Location: Dick's Auto Sales and Rebuilding,
Mound House, Nevada

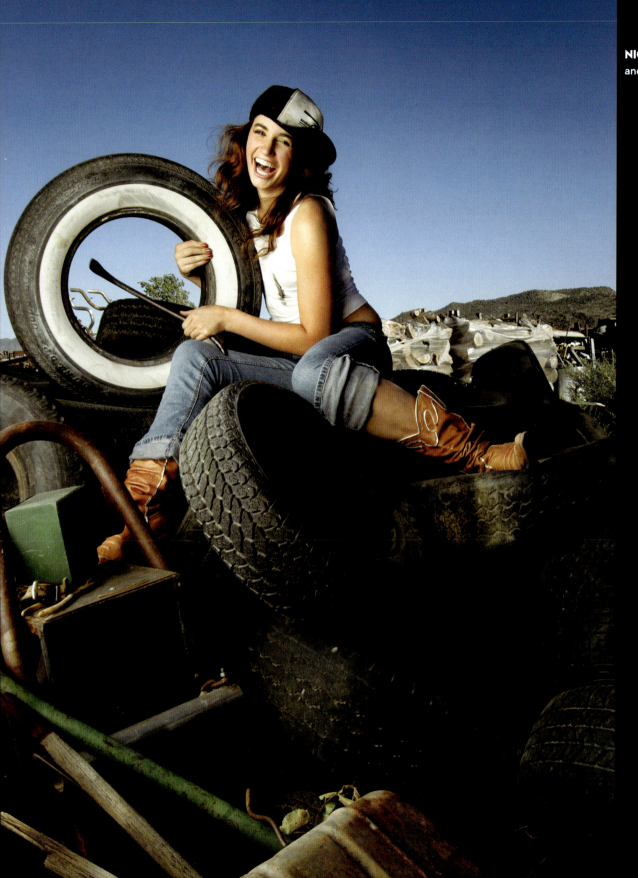

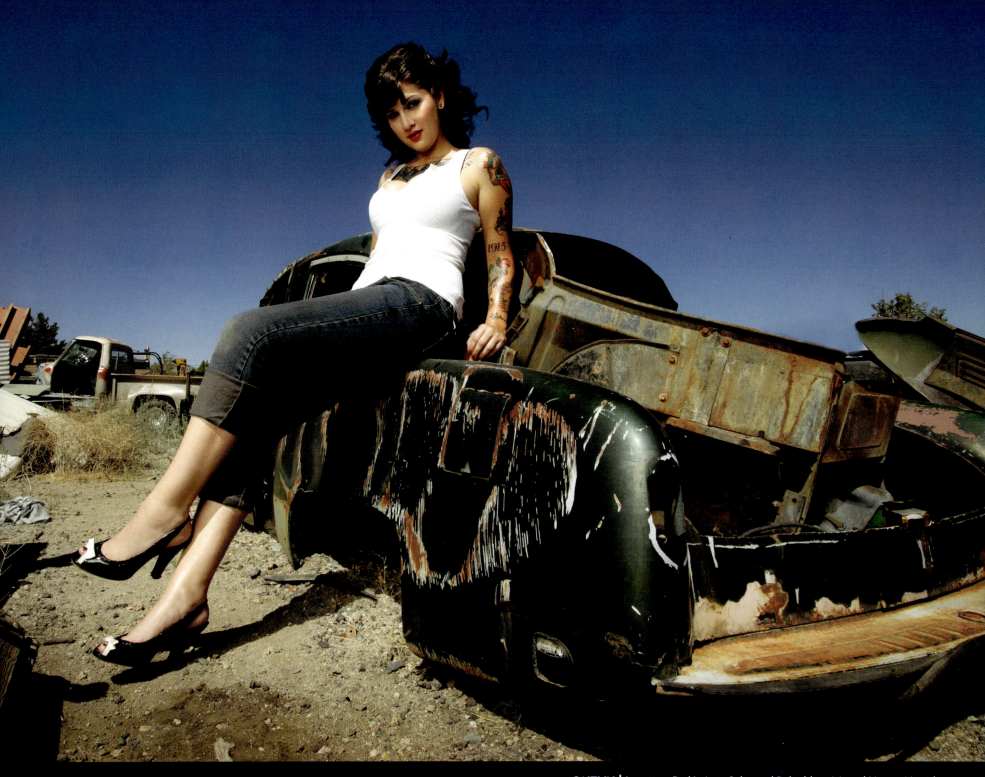

CAITLIN | Location: Dick's Auto Sales and Rebuilding, Mound House, Nevada

Derby Doll Caitlin finds the perfect trim piece and pistons for her sled.

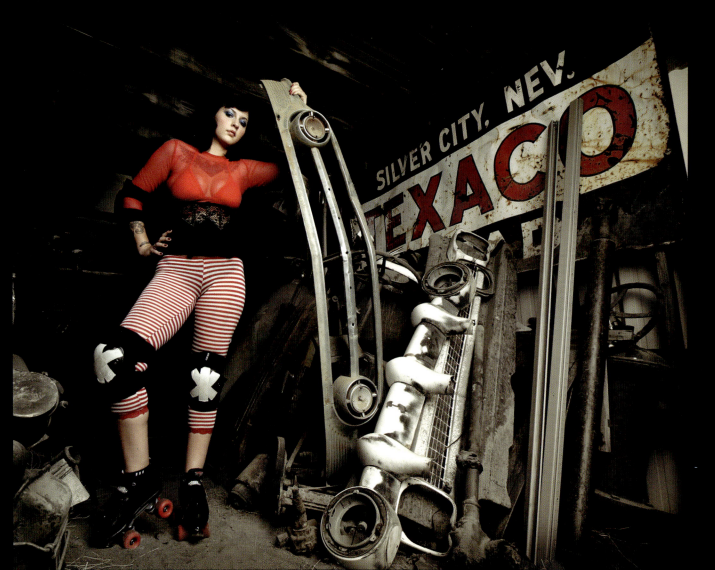

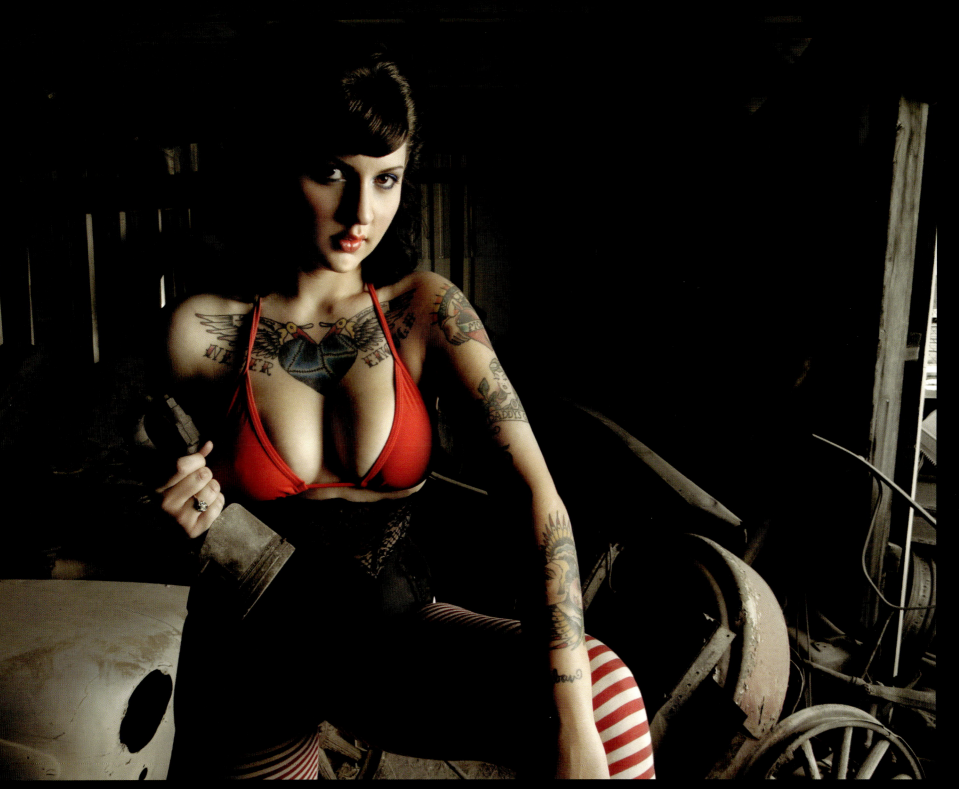

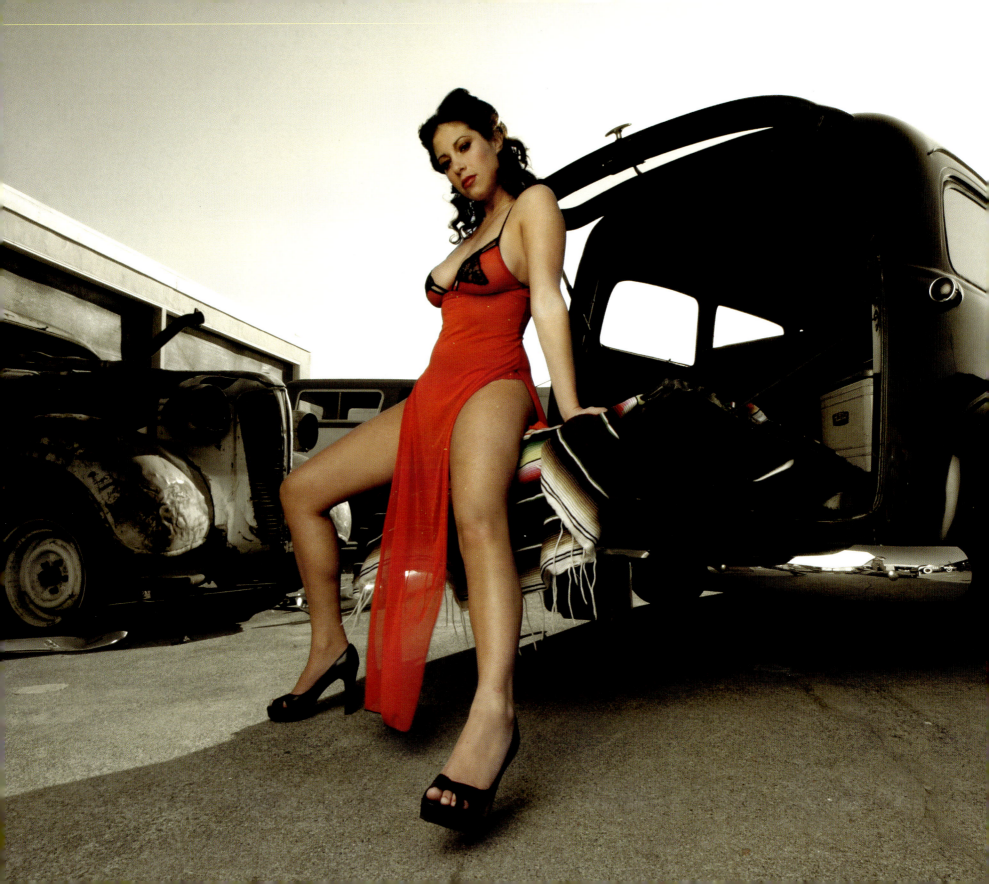

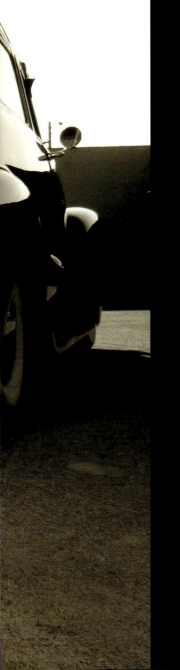

LARK | 1948 Chevy Suburban | Owner: Ezio Siri | Location: Vallejo, California

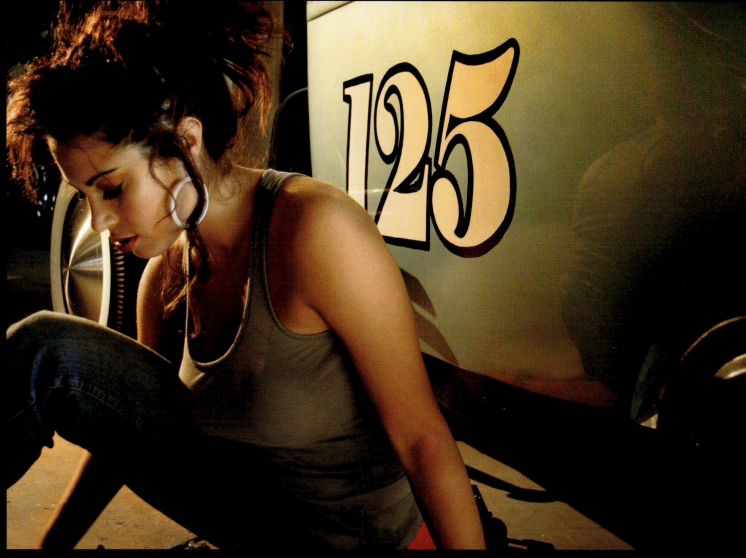

LARK | 1927 Ford Model A | Owner: Matt Seret | Location: Vallejo, California

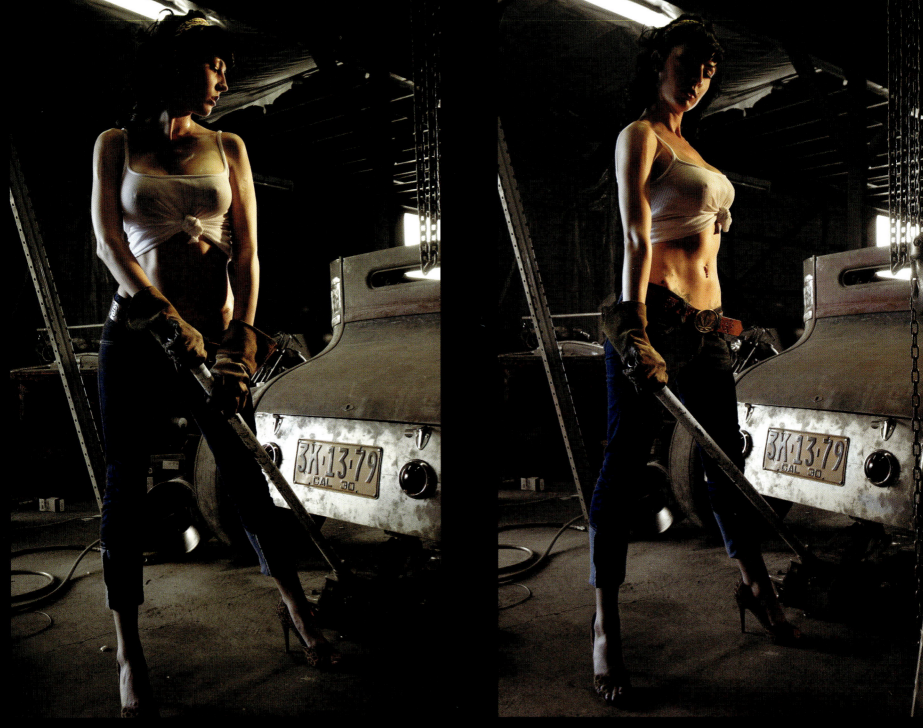

RUBY | 1927 Model T Ford | Owner: Matt Seret | Location: Seret Customs, Vallejo, California

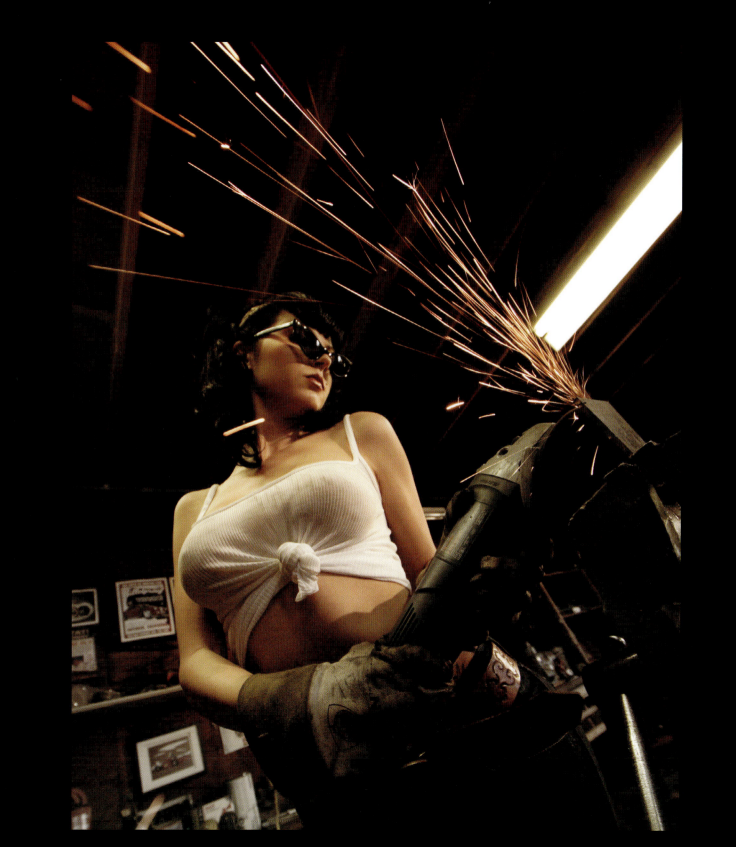

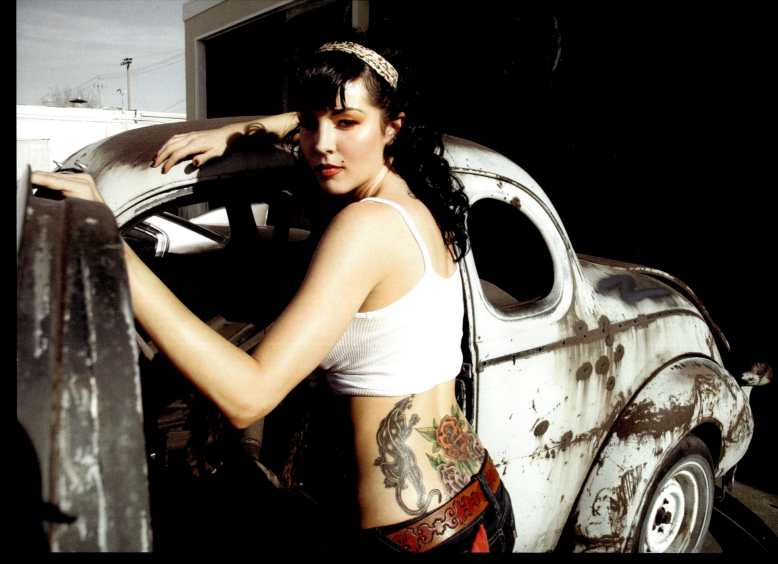

RUBY | 1937 Plymouth Five-Window | Owner: Matt Seret | Location: Seret Customs, Vallejo, California

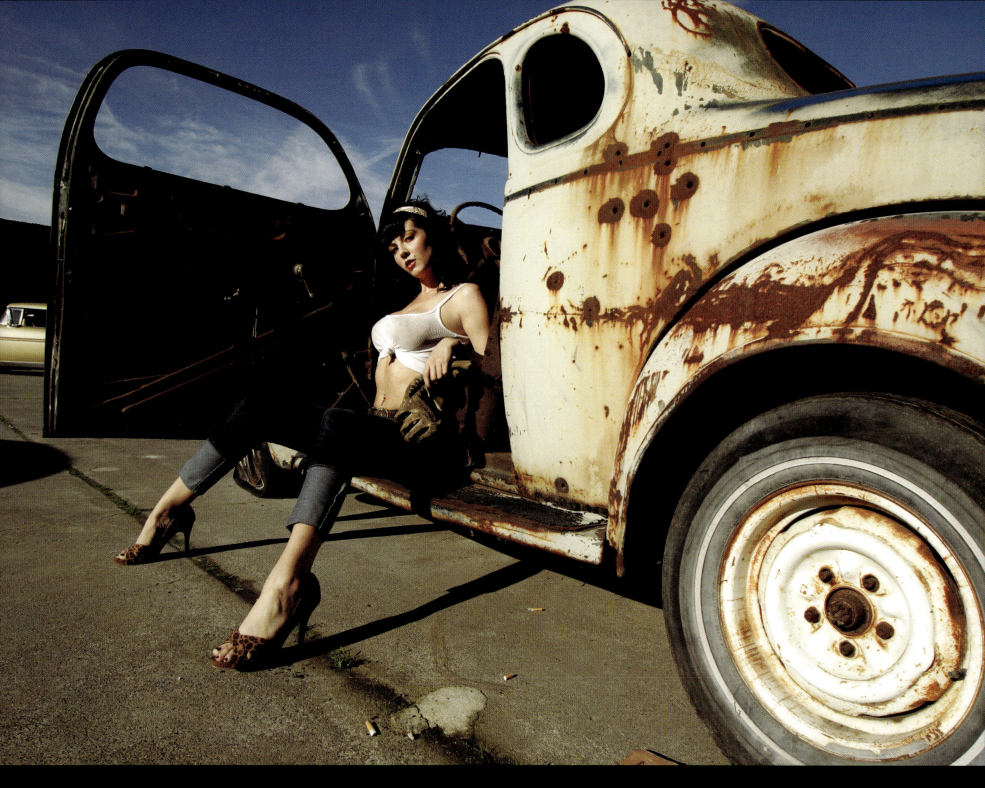

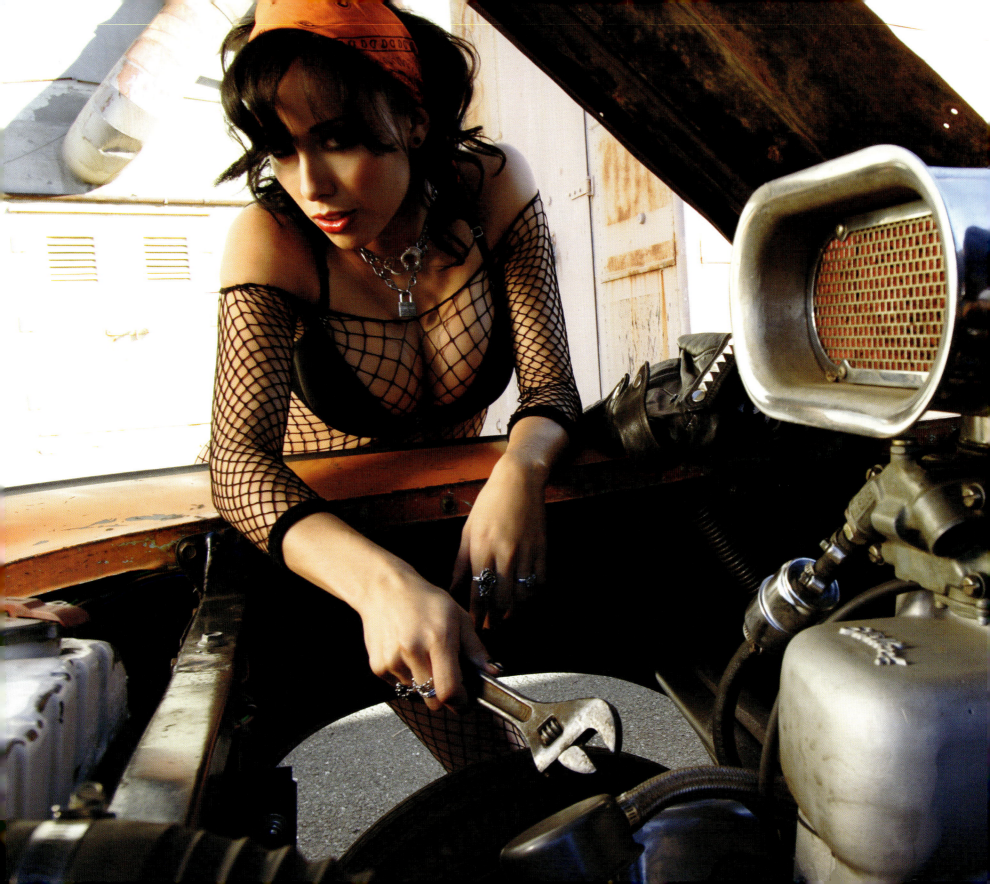

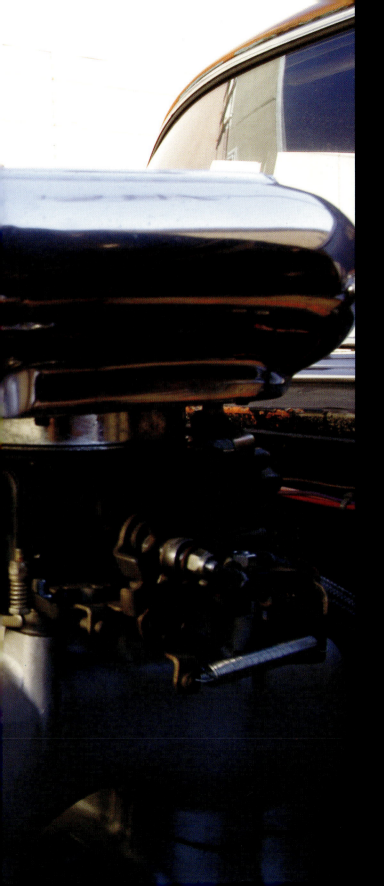

dragstrips, dry lakes and dirt tracks

Damn that Jimmy! The jalopy was a bear. The tracking must have been out—again. Every lap of the trophy dash he'd had to fight it to keep ahead of the pack, but off to the side he could see flashes of black and white as the checkered flag swirled. Another win. Another kiss from the trophy queen—it was every man's dream. But tonight Connie was the winner in more ways than one.

Trophy queens didn't typically go home with the racer—they had more sense than that—but Connie knew this one would. They had been secretly married only the week before and, if he had his way, this would be her last appearance before a crowd in what to him was little more than her underwear—a bikini, to be exact. The crowd loved her though, and only a fool would think that they were cheering the winner—they were cheering those legs that reached all the way from the ground to, well, her peach of an ass.

I'm getting ahead of myself though. The relationship between Connie and Donna could be traced way back to the early days of the bicycle, when sex was used not only to sell two-wheeled freedom to women but also to convince men that they could meet women while out bicycling. It worked. Bicycle sales went through the roof. In fact, this rather obvious marketing strategy worked so well that the fledgling automobile industry adopted it wholeheartedly and eventually pushed it to the limits of propriety.

Art came around to the start. Flash bulbs popped and crackled as he grabbed the flag and made a lap of honor, hanging out of the window like a drive-in tray while giving it gas. The engine popped. The steering was almost nonexistent. Connie could see pink. Donna was standing on the little wooden podium next to CJ, the promoter. She looked ice-cream-sundae delicious in her damn pink bikini and cherry lips.

Connie always thought it was funny that he'd fallen for Donna. He'd had his pick of the litter, especially before the war, when he won a local Jitterbug Championship. Heck, he'd even danced with Bette Davis in the movie *Thank Your Lucky Stars*. Bette wasn't his type, though. Donna was. Donna was a down-to-earth gal with great assets.

After another squirrelly lap, Connie pulled over and jumped out of the car, only just remembering to knock it out of gear. He jumped up on the podium, taking Donna in his arms and squeezing her tight, taking the trophy and whispering, "Last race!" In his excitement he didn't notice her tense ever so slightly. The crowd roared as Connie swung around and tossed the trophy in the air. He felt CJ's hand

slide down Donna's butt and he struck it hard like a rattlesnake. The hand flinched away in pained surprise.

Connie had hugged them all, from Balboa up the coast to Gardena Bowl, even the Coliseum, but he liked the smaller tracks such as Balboa best. He'd even hugged nineteen-year-old Raquel Tejada once—she went on to become Raquel Welch—but Donna was the best. She'd been Miss Temple City and he'd first seen her in a magazine draped over the rear fender of Marcia Campbell's '49 Chevy. He never thought he'd marry her, though. Her legs were as long and tapered as a Barris fadeaway, and her hair was as blonde as Marilyn's, but Donna was cuter. She was a bombshell all right. Hydrogen bombshell! Hollywood material, they said. In fact, she'd auditioned just the week before over at Paramount. She'd done pretty well, she thought. Of course, all that would stop now that they were married.

In the pits, Connie laid into Jimmy about the steering. "It needs more toe. The damn thing steers like a stuck pig." Jimmy said he'd fix it as soon as he got himself a Coke. Of course, Connie knew that "Coke" meant a good shot of Jack, but what the heck, they only had the main event to go and they had a pretty good chance of getting in the money. They'd won the trophy dash, and that was good.

When he climbed into the car for the main event, they were all there. "Big Bill." He owned the car. All the hangers-on. Then there was Donna. A flamingo in the pits. No sign of Jimmy, though.

Suddenly, it was time to go. Connie yanked down on his goggles and took off, spitting gravel, hoping to heck it showered CJ. Slime ball. Always gawking at Donna like she was . . . well? Whatever.

In his anger, Connie cut out, gunnin' it hard until he found his place. He knew it wasn't going to be so easy this time. But a little nitro in the tank would make all the difference in the world. And who'd know? Nobody.

As soon as the flag dropped, Connie found himself wrestling two monkeys in a grease pit. Jimmy hadn't even *looked* at the damn steering. Gol darn it. It was easier once he was in the groove and he managed to keep out in front. Eventually, the last-lap flag flashed by. He made the turn. On the infield, there was Donna, stepping up onto the podium. You can bet that slimy CJ was giving her a hand—on the ass. He pulled hard on the wheel, angry at the thought as the car careened out of control. He remembered the screen turning pink—cherry smeared across her face—as Donna bounced over the hood of his car—CJ holding her hand. Two rag dolls out on their last date.

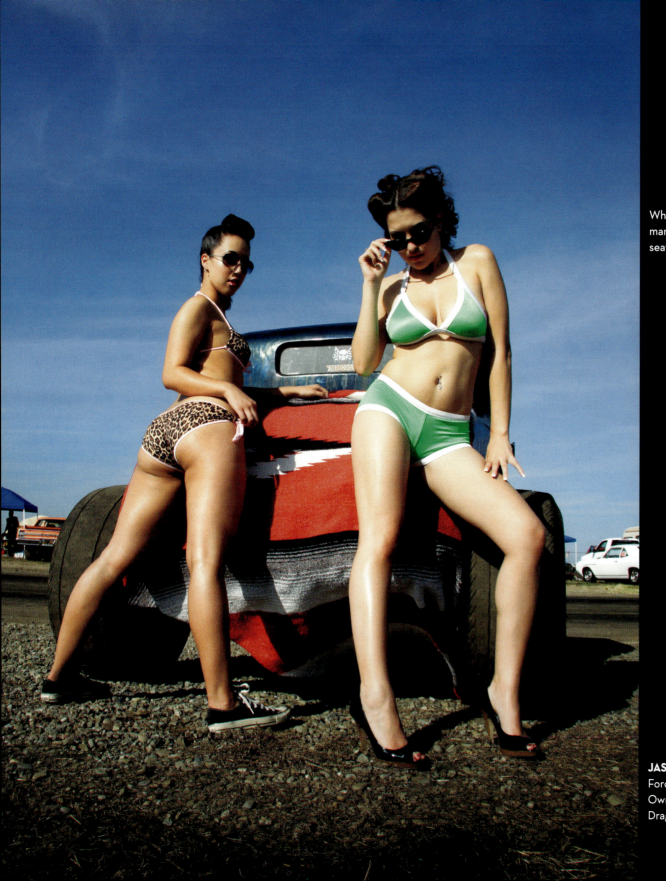

While muggin', Jasmine and Crystal manage to avoid the scalding rumble seat of Scott Mugford's Model A.

JASMINE & CRYSTAL | 1928 Model A Ford Five-Window the *Bluegrass Express* Owner: Scott Mugford | Location: Kingdon Drags, Lodi, California

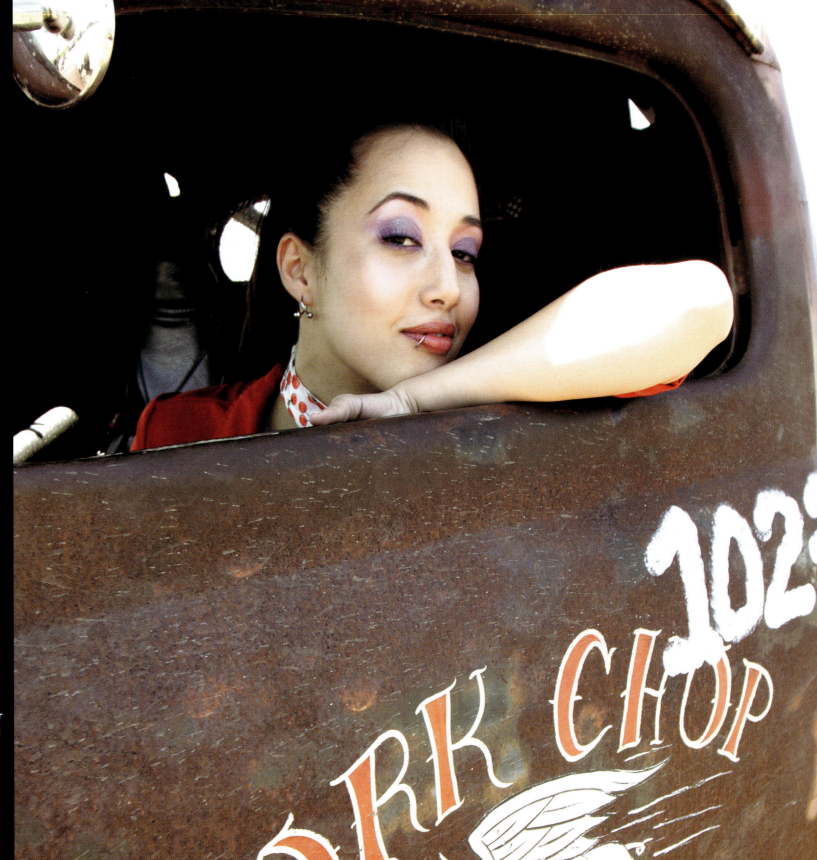

Jasmine fat-arms in Chris'
Pork Chop Special at the
Kingdon Drags.

JASMINE | 1949 Ford F1
with 283 bored 0.060 over
Owner: Chris Sommerfeld
Location: Kingdon Drags,
Lodi, California

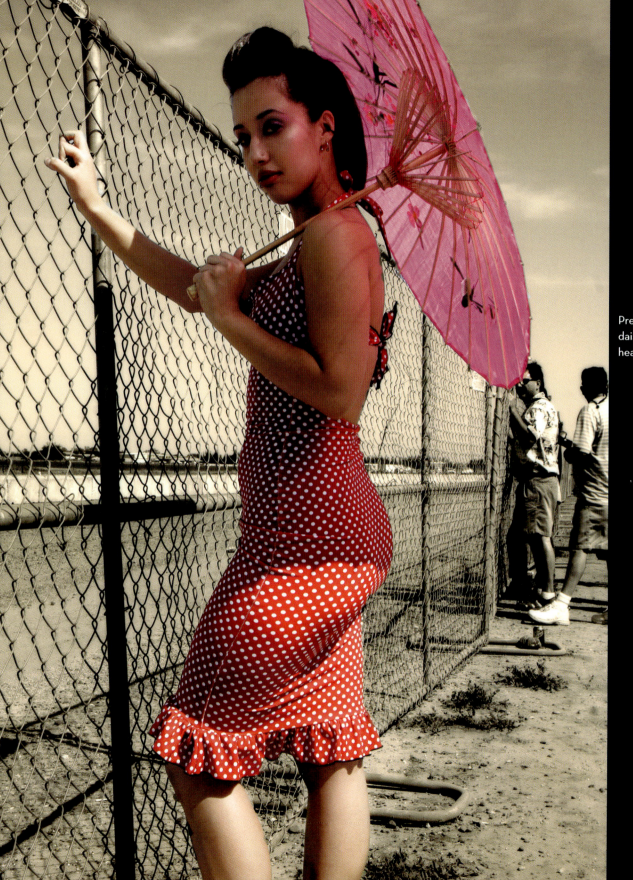

Pretty in pink and fresh as a daisy, Jasmine beats the Lodi heat with her pink parasol.

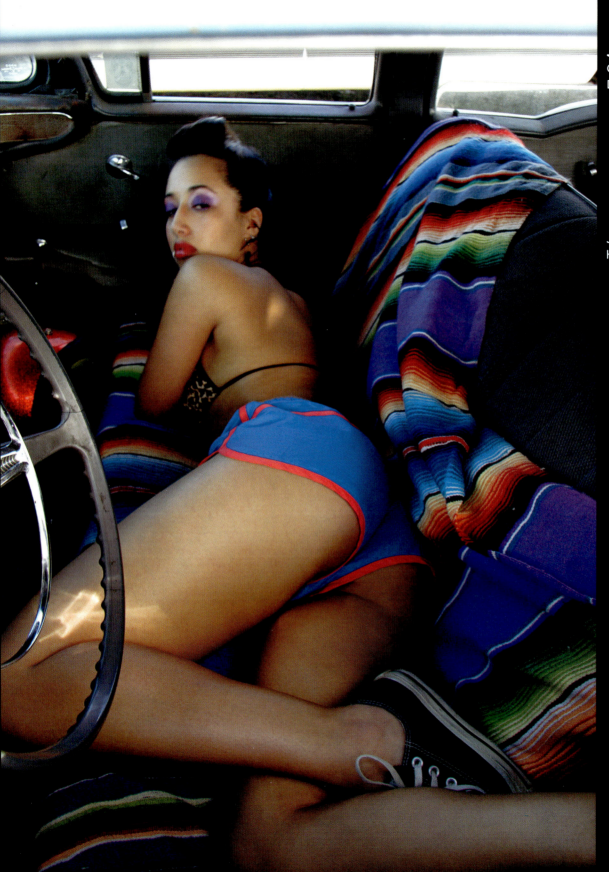

JASMINE | 1958 Buick Yeoman Wagon
Owner: Rob Cannon | Location: Kingdon
Drags, Lodi, California

Jasmine peeps and pouts in the sweltering
heat at the Kingdon Drags.

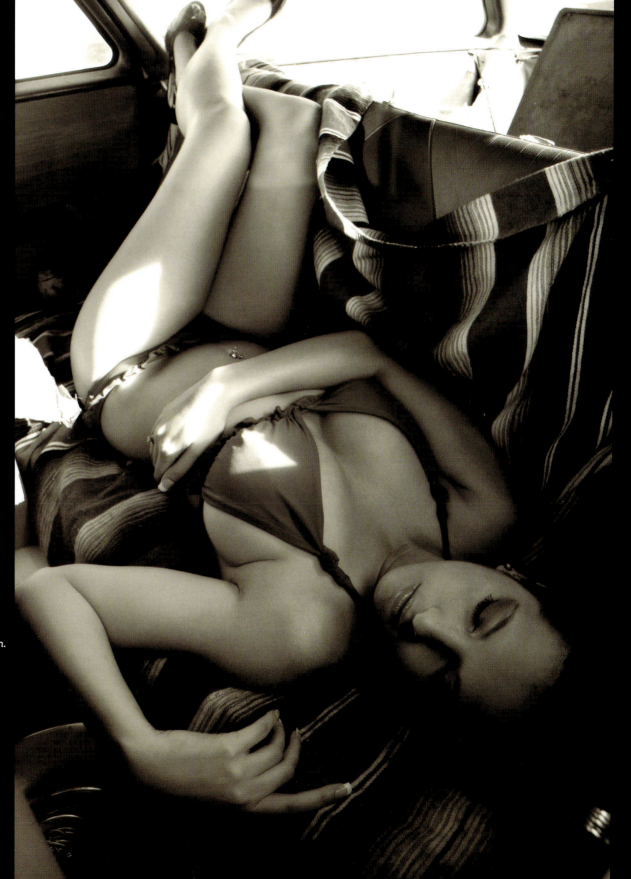

After a long day of struttin' and posin', Crystal dreams of Top Fuel eliminations in the back of Rob Cannon's 1958 Buick, *The Draggin' Waggin*.

CRYSTAL | 1958 Buick Yeoman Wagon
Owner: Rob Cannon | Location: Kingdon Drags, Lodi, California

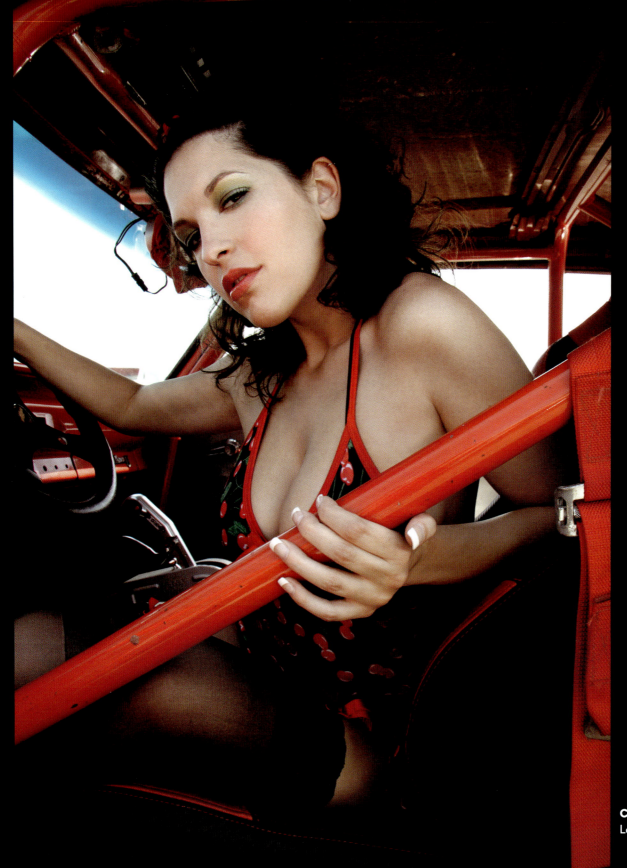

CRYSTAL | 1962 Chevy Nova | Owner: Joe Blow
Location: Kingdon Drags, Lodi, California

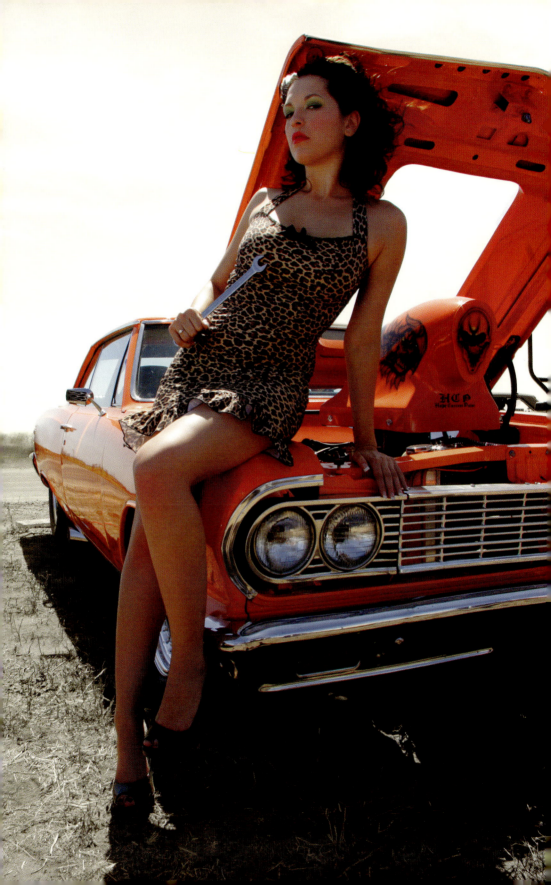

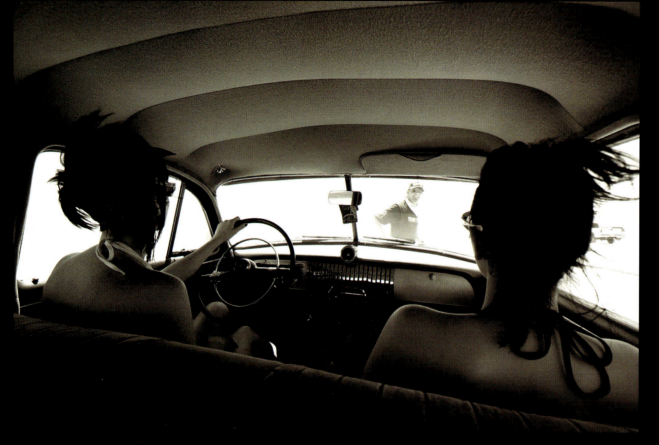
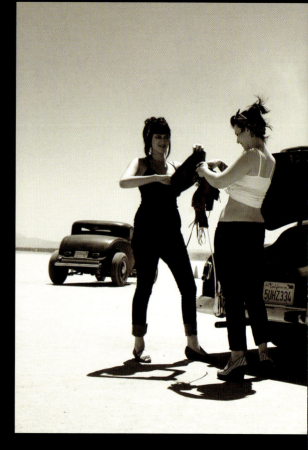

MORGAN & GIAVONNA | 1951 Chevy & 1932 Ford Three-Window | Owners: Giovanna & Doug Bosse | Location: El Mirage

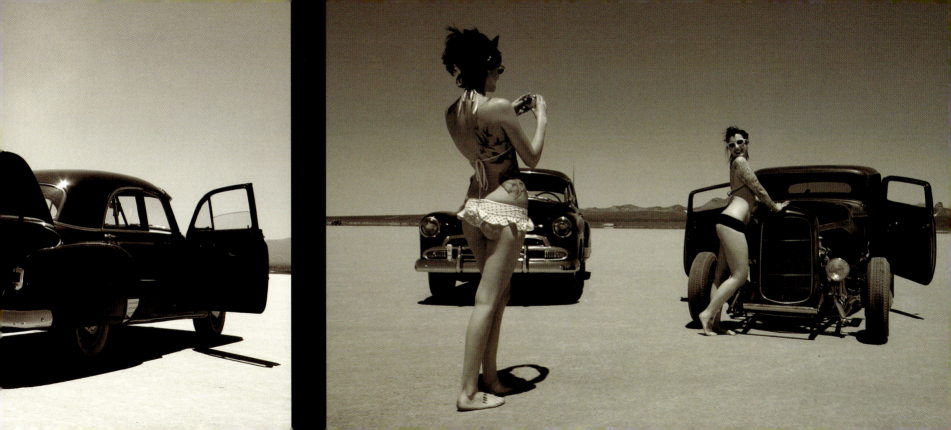

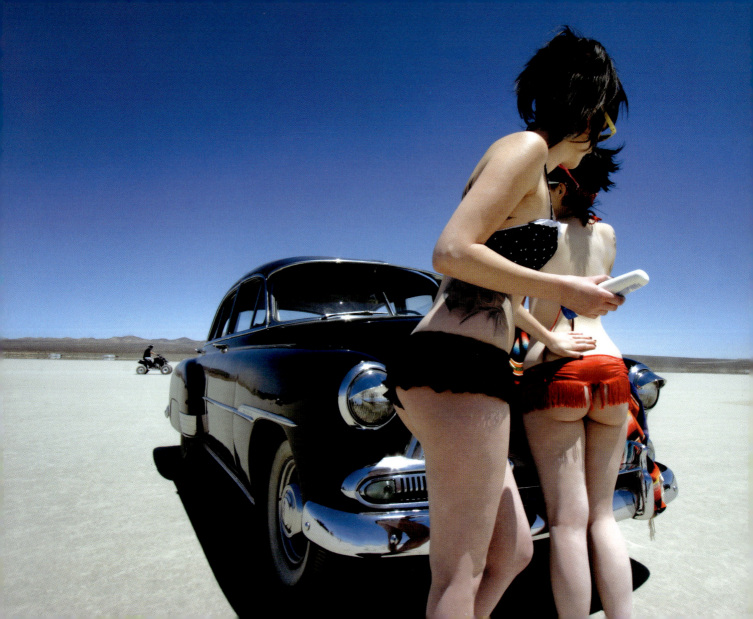

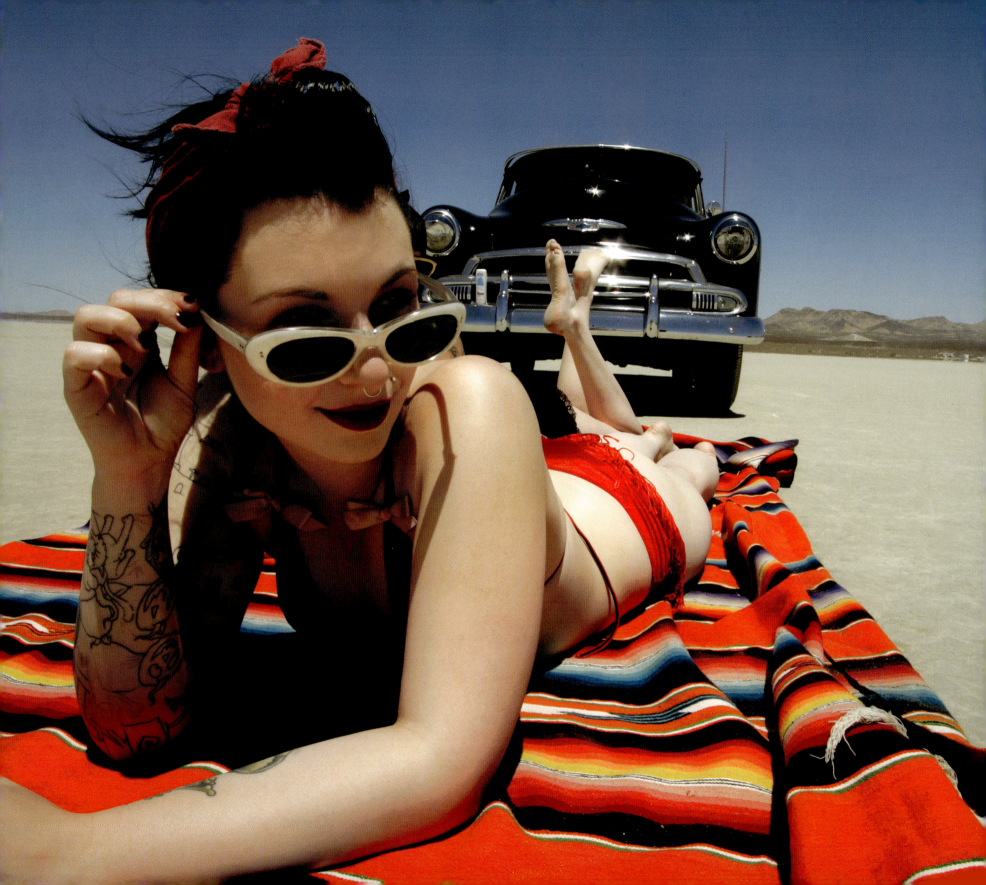

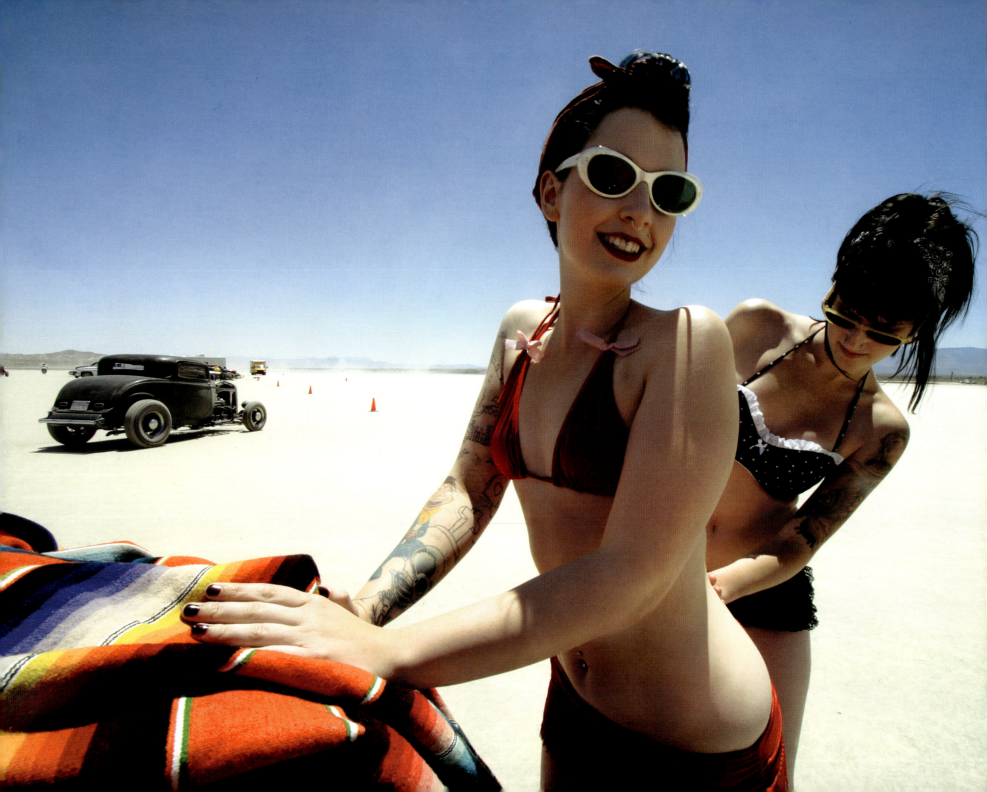

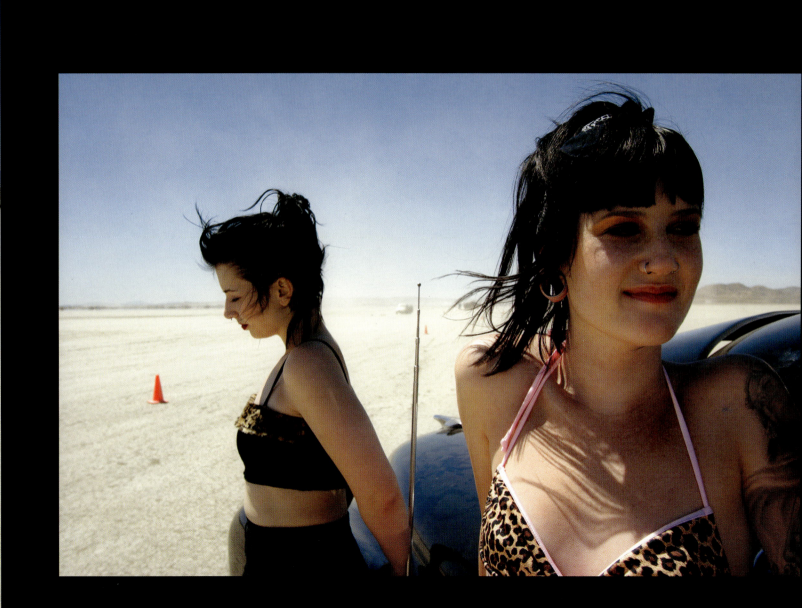

Teresa tinkers and titillates under the hood and in the back seat, respectively, of Gunar's Tri-Chev with history. The '57 was raced by the team of Ed and Pat George from Turlock, California in the '60s and early '70s. Ed built the engines . . . wife Pat did the driving.

TERESA | Ed's Automotive and Speed 1957 Chevy Bel Air | Owner: Gunar Hansken
Club: Swanx | Location: Historic Arsenal, Benicia, California

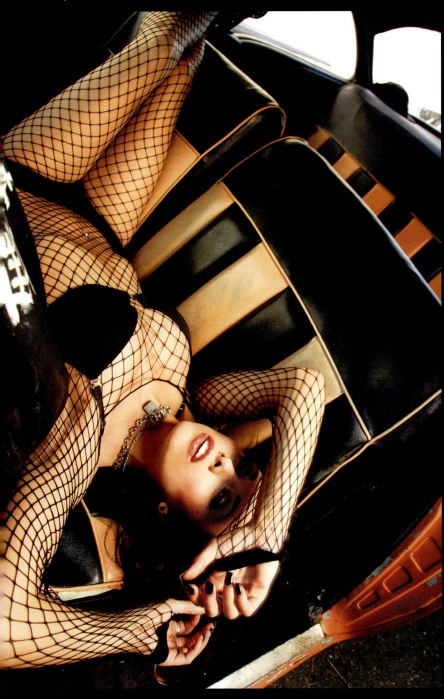

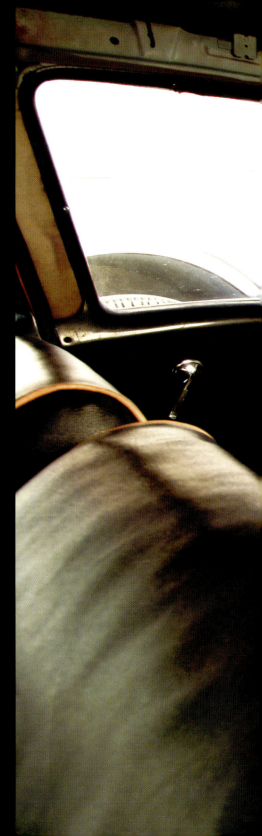

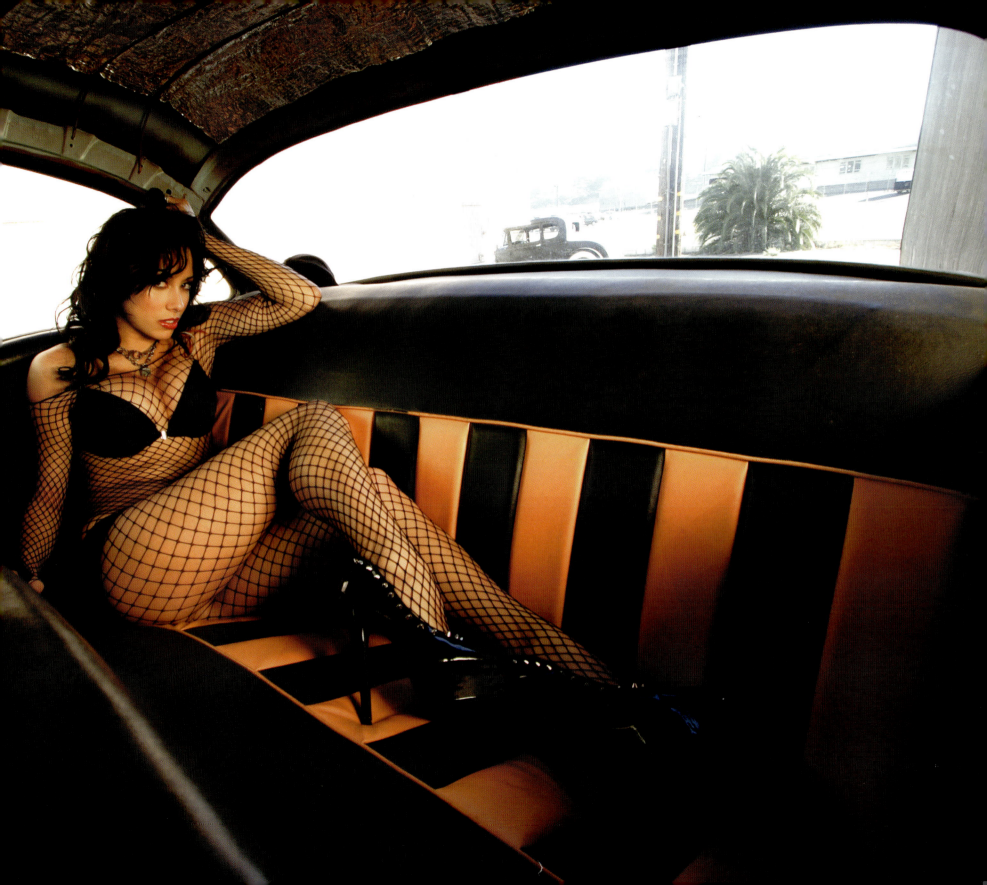

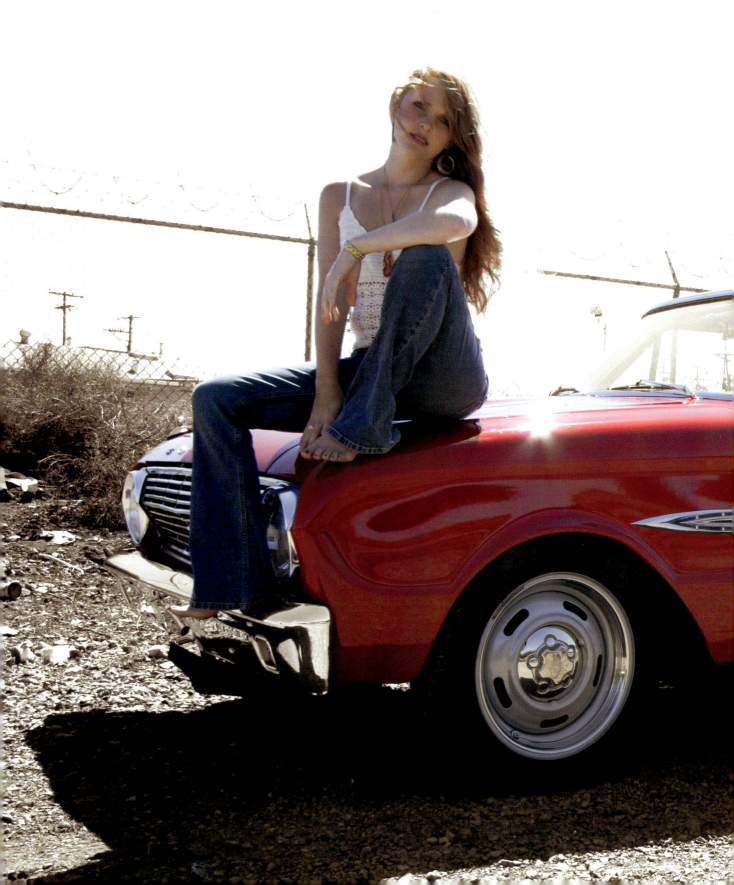

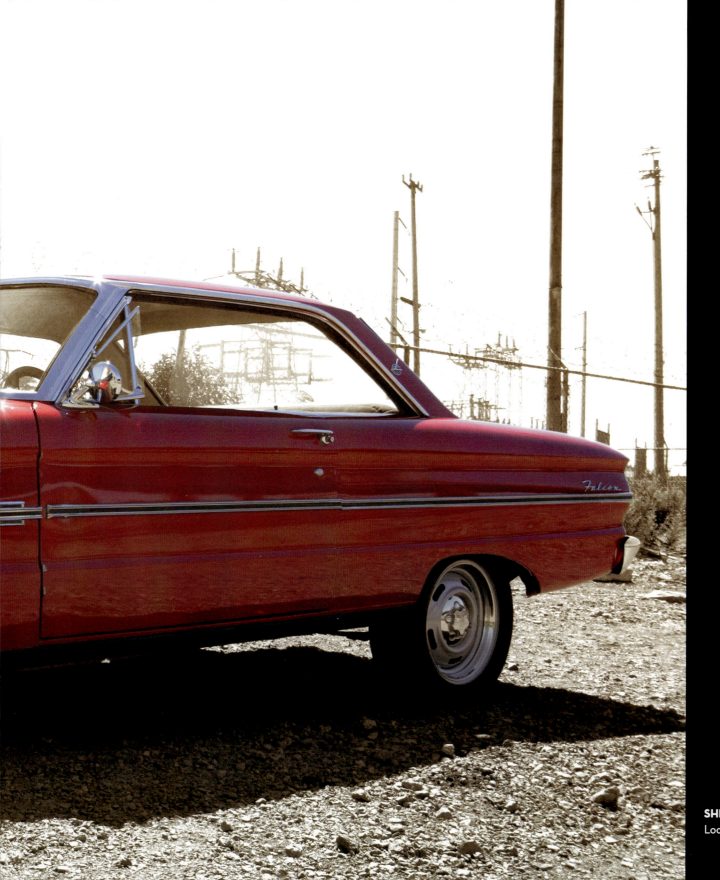

SHELLEY | 1963 Ford Falcon | Owner: Jason Cole
Location: Richmond, California

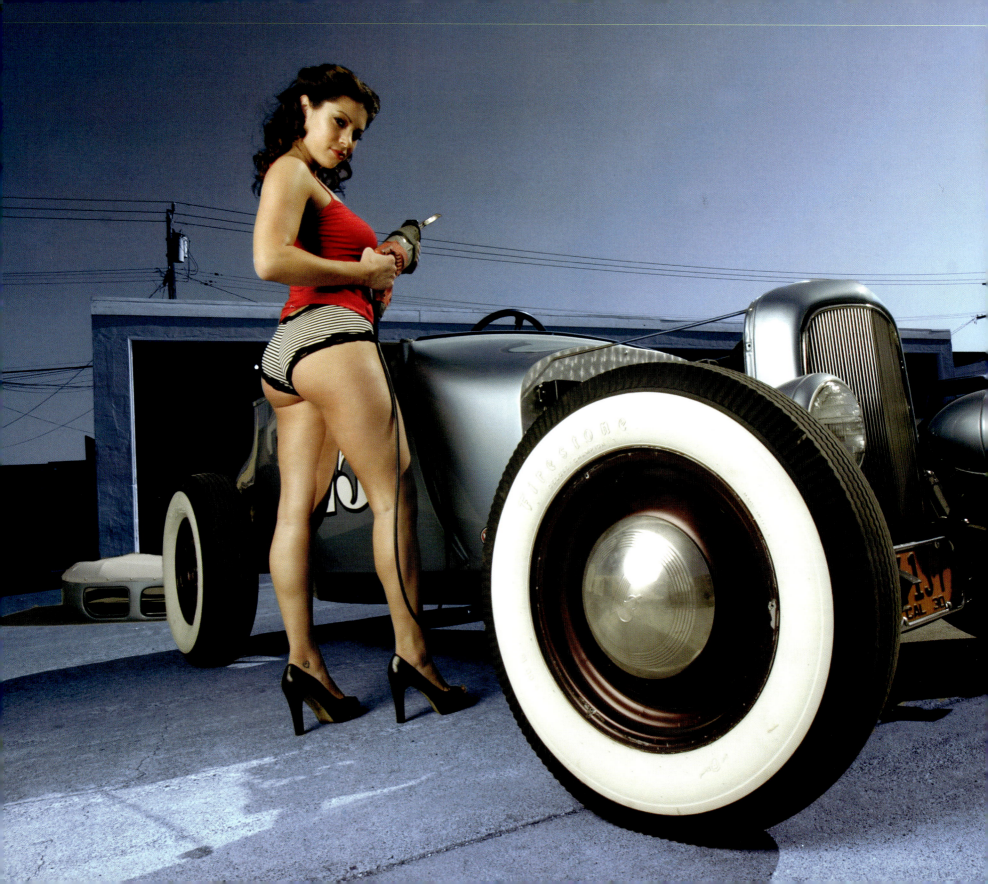

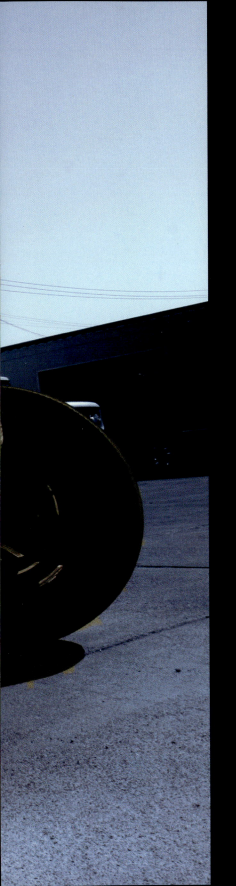

LARK | 1927 Ford Model A | Owner: Matt Seret | Location: Vallejo, California

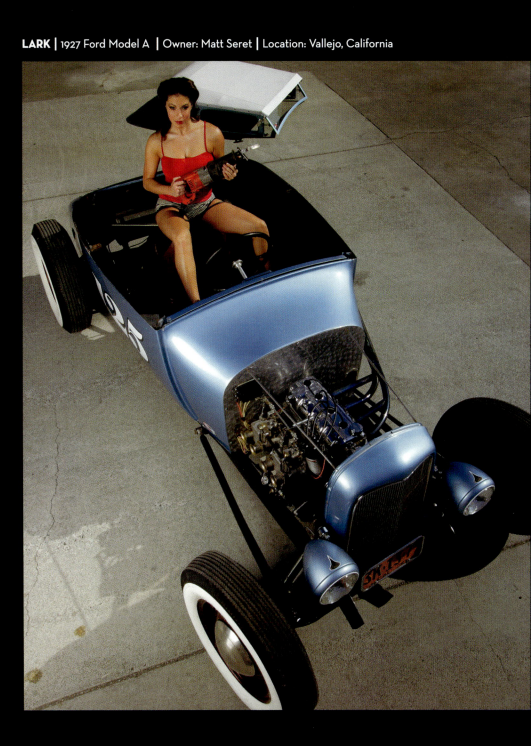

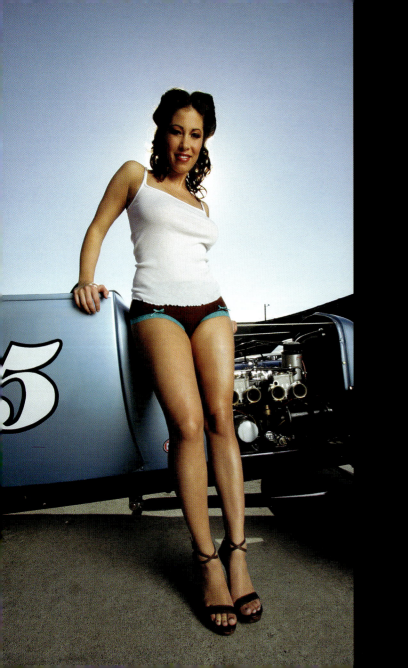
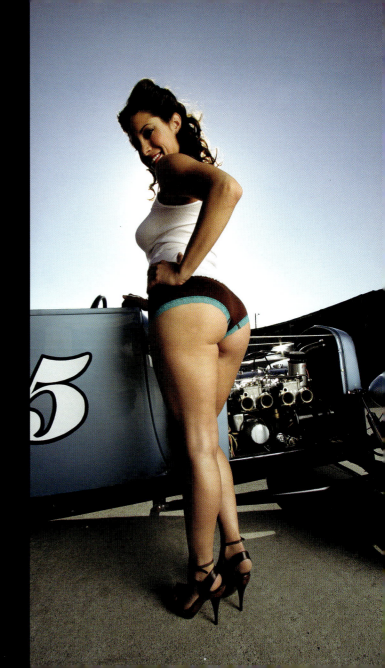

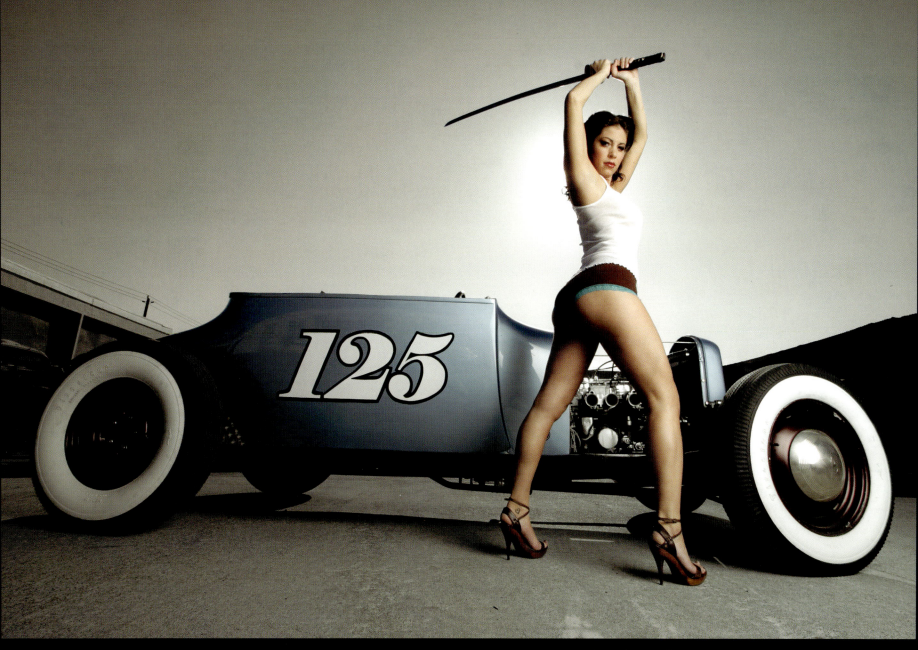

Kamikaze cutie Lark chops the top off Matt's coupe, settin' the purists' tongues a-waggin'.

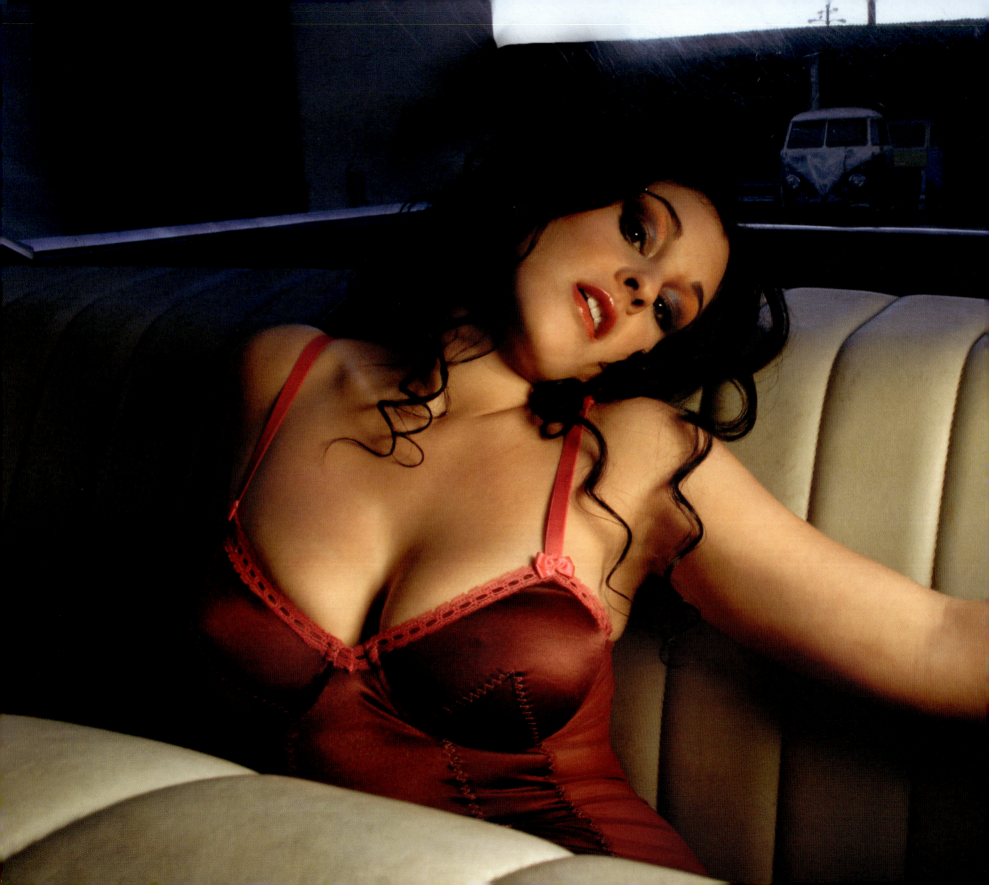

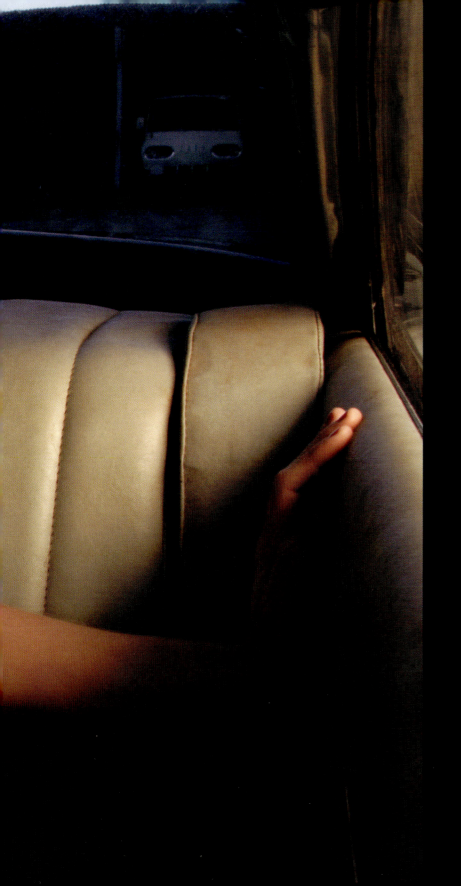

down on the street

It was the first night of the new moon in October. Even though light fog had come to the valleys, the land was dry and the night was warm. A low trail of fine dust rose in the red glow of the taillights of a car moving slowly downgrade. The dust disappeared into the ink of night as the car crept along, giving it the impression of being powered by roiling phantoms pushing from behind. In the dim of hooded fog lamps, trees reared alongside the road, and tall grasses shadowed a thousand shadows in the lights.

The driver wore a beat Resistol over her jet black hair. In the dim light from the dash, her skin appeared luminous and the sinew in her long arms shifted as she guided the car around the bends. Her lean frame reclined in the bucket seat. She was calmly smoking and listening to a new 8-track tape of Neil Young singing "Are you ready for the country?" A chuckle rose and a jet of smoke escaped her lips when she thought of the irony of it all, as she headed due south to the highway and the city. When she thought of the title of the album she was listening to, she laughed out loud in the way she reserved for herself and few others to hear.

It had been years since she left behind the cold mitten of Michigan and the laughter shared with a young man who was dead before his time. She took his car, a 1965 Buick Skylark with a twin quad 425, and headed west. It was the car that had brought them together right out of high school. Back then he was a hopped-up adrenaline junkie with a brand new car, and she was a beautiful loner into trouble.

They were fuel for each other's fire right from the start, and the Buick was under their hands whenever their hands weren't on each other. Street racing became their livelihood. They painted the heavily muffled sleeper black with spray cans and took on all comers in towns throughout the state. Frances "Frankie" Anglin was quick to learn, and her quick reflexes and light weight made her the ideal driver. As their notoriety grew, so did the young man's habit, until the day he turned blue in the summer of '67 on the shore of Lake Huron.

She went home and did nothing for a year, until what she kept inside herself became unbearable. With fifty bucks and a tank of gas, she idled out of the motor court and never looked back. She raced burger joint chumps along U.S. 40 and down 95 to Vegas. For six months she worked the tables by day and at night put her long legs and lithe body to work at the burlesque shows, until her bottled emotions became unbearable again and she hit the road.

She floated like a ghost in the night on the edges of LA, living in the Skylark. Her hands were burnt, her knuckles torn. Her hair was long black straw she kept under a gimme cap. Her beauty had become downright feral. Venturing into town only to race, she took them down in Compton and up on Mullholland. All day long she slept off the adrenaline and pills, while her vortex slowly headed north. When she finally stopped long enough to get a read on her compass, her grey eyes were bloodshot and pouring tears into a basket of fries on the Great Highway next to the Pacific Ocean. San Francisco was right behind her, alive with light and people, but it was dead for her.

The next morning she sat in the parking lot next to the Golden Gate Bridge counting her money. Her frugal and winning ways amounted to just about a grand. A greasy map she lifted from a service station a year before was spread across the tired upholstery. Far north of Point Reyes lay the "Lost Coast." That sounded good to her. After all, where was she if she was not lost? "Well, Frances, you might as well be lost and get it done in one place," she reasoned. Then she headed over the bridge into the early air of the fall of 1970.

Upon arrival it was clear she could not stay. There was no street racing and no place to get a job, and the weather had turned decidedly wet. She found a job cleaning hotel rooms in the Redwoods, but as winter closed in there were few tourists to clean up after and she was let go. Waitressing in Garberville netted little cash and the constant grabass from the boss pissed her off. Again she headed south.

In a bar in Laytonville, Frank Post wore a thousand-yard stare while he listened to his friends bullshitting. He was completely trapped in the beauty of a woman he had never seen before. She was wearing boots under a faded pair of Levis and a worn flannel shirt that was open enough to reveal her perfect skin cleaving away under the breast pockets. Frank was getting glassy. In this dream state he got off his barstool and followed his gaze over to Frankie. He walked right up

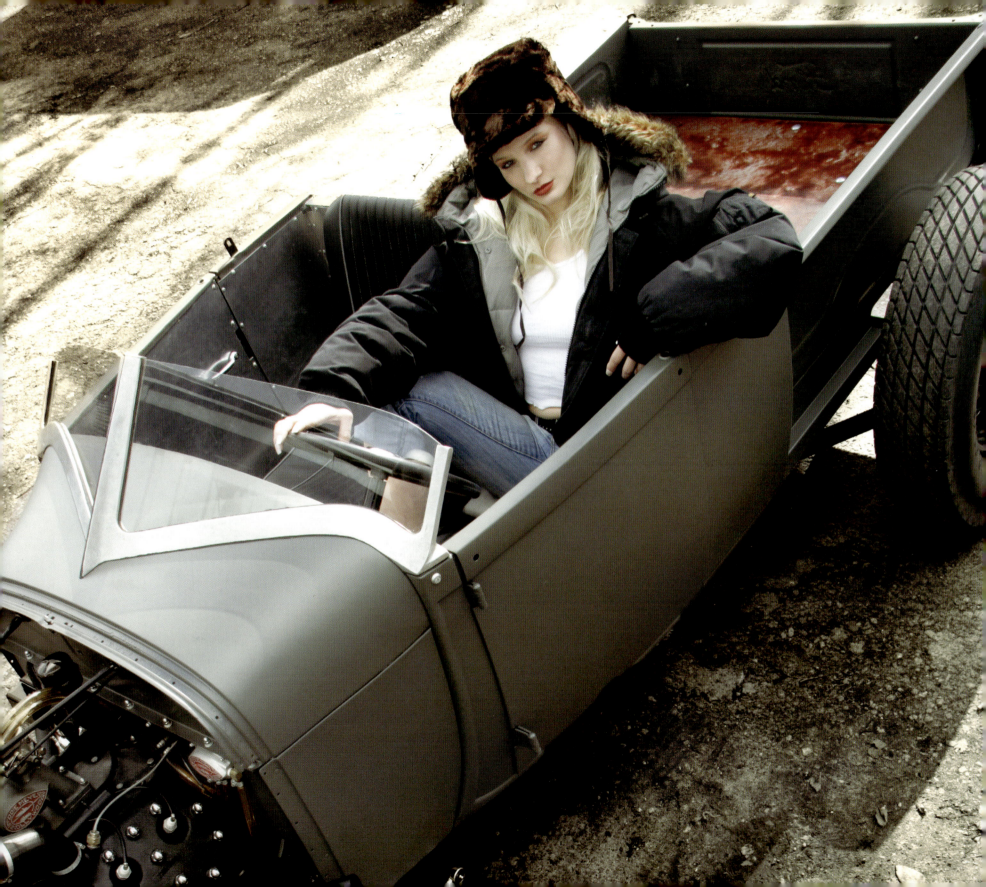

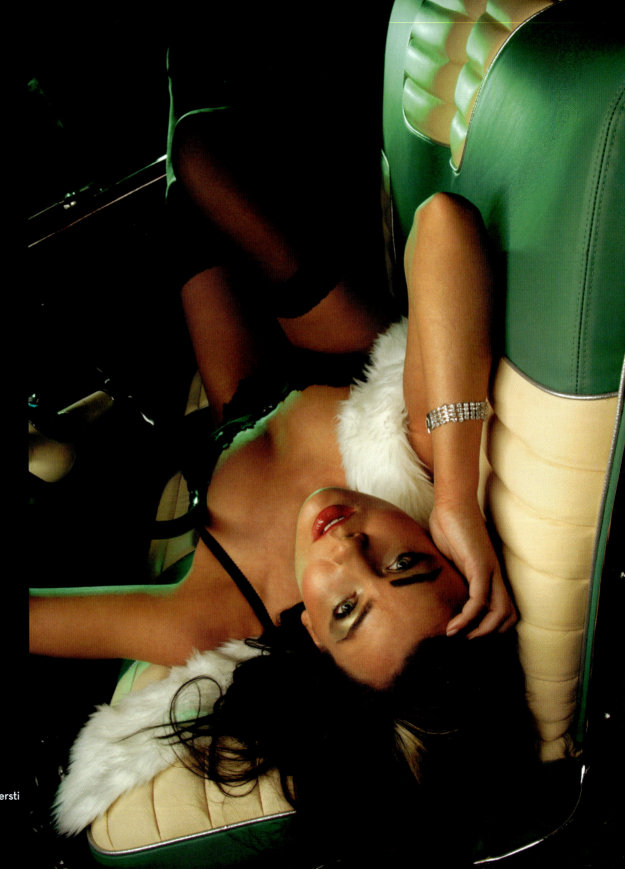

NIINA | 1941 Lincoln Zephyr | Owner: Timo Hersti
Club: Recyclers | Location: Hyrylä, Finland

...to her as if he had always known her and asked, "You wanna get outta here?" She looked up at a pair of green eyes, smiled, and ran a finger around the edge of the ashtray before saying "Yeah, I do." "C'mon then," he said, and Frankie followed Frank out the door into the rain.

They didn't say a word as he climbed into a pickup and she started up the Skylark. They drove until the pavement ended and then drove some more. The road disintegrated the farther they went and she fought with the wheel and the gas to keep up with the truck around hideous hairpins loose with running water. She nearly drove up onto the bed of the pickup as she crested a rise. Nothing made sense anymore, and just what the hell was she doing out here in the rain, following a handsome and possibly psychotic stranger? She got out of the car in a rage. Her fury went straight to the cab and unleashed for a few seconds before she felt a tap on her shoulder. "We're here," he said. Frankie slowly turned and melted into Frank with a kiss that had waited three years to be given.

The two became so inseparable that everyone in town called them "the Franks." Frank swore he'd never met one like her and never would again. For Frankie it seemed like the past had changed into something new and alive. They lived off what they grew for the eager counter-culture in the cities. Shacked up by the fire in winter, planting in March, making love in the creek in the summer, harvesting in the fall, and then driving to "Frisco" with a full load. Of course Frankie did the driving.

She never really needed to use her skills anymore, and for fun she kept in shape by becoming a master of the dirt. She'd bounce into Willits at 5 A.M. and hose the brown dirt off the car behind a gas station. In the restroom she'd paint her wide mouth a deep red, and put on a pair of low-heeled shoes and a knee-length skirt. Then she'd put her long black hair up into a flower print scarf, fill up, and hit the road looking square as could be. By the time she hit San Francisco it was the morning rush and she blended right in, no one the wiser for the load she was carrying. It had been close once in Hopland, but she killed the lights and dusted the poor deputy right off. When she could no longer see his lights in the rearview she laughed that laugh of hers until it turned into a choking cry.

She thought it had gone away for good but there it was again. A pain deep inside for which there was no succor. Her initial response was flight, and after she dumped the load, she fisted the cash and was in San Jose before she caught hold of herself and turned around.

Running wasn't an option anymore. She beat the daylights out of the car until she was home safe in the woods, asleep in Frank's arms.

She passed it off but she wasn't the same. A flood was rising inside of her despite her struggle to contain it. Frank was bewildered and poured his heart all over her, to no avail. Frankie's practice drives became more frequent and often at night. She'd come home with her face caked in dust, drink a bottle of wine and collapse. For a week, maybe two, she'd be the same old Frankie, but her clouds were gathering. Her moods became impenetrable to Frank.

She became more careless on her runs. Slipping into Willits for fuel she no longer bothered with the hose and once ran up and down Ukiah until the one cop on duty was forced to wake up and attempt to chase her. She'd raise hell by the houseboats in Sausalito and then get lost in the traffic. It was only a matter of time. More than one small-town cop was looking to bust her, and the CHP was hot for her too.

So it was under a moonless sky in October of '72. She was on a high, gently guiding the Skylark and its payload toward the highway. Taking it easy, she stopped on top of one her favorite hills. She parked the car in the middle of the road and let it idle, opened the door and stepped out. It was clear, and even in the dark she could see the ocean moving far off to the west. Behind her the Skylark loped quietly in a deep bass. The sound of it turned her thoughts to Lake Huron, and she could feel it ebbing against her chest. She thought of his face and the love she still held tightly. She turned off the car and let the night sounds creep up on her.

Falling into the fractal sway of their harmonies, she dreamt. When she woke she rubbed the images from her eyes and walked over to the car, popped the hood, lifted the air cleaner and threw it into the brush. Gently she pushed the throttle until the second carb began to open and then jammed her pocketknife into the gap. She opened the door, got in and placed the shifter in neutral, tied a length of rope around it and started the car. It fired and then stalled. Again she twisted the key and it came on, quiet except for the air rushing down the carburetors. She got out, stepped back, and held the rope. "Fuck it," she said and pulled hard on the rope. The Skylark went berserk down the hill. About fifty yards out, it left the road and began plowing down brush. It caught a little air, gently tipped nose down, and then hit hard; it ran for a little while longer, and died. Frankie ran her sleeve across her face, worked the dust with her boot and started walking.

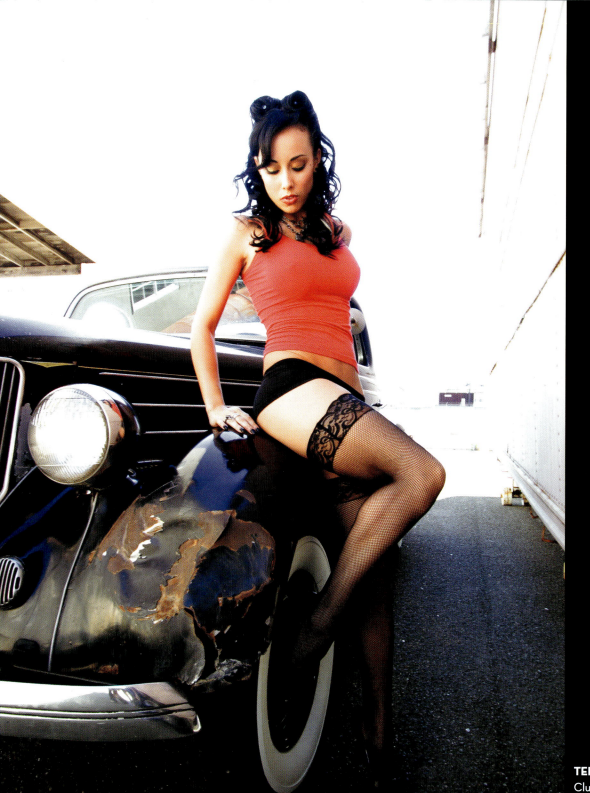

TERESA | 1936 Ford Three-Window | Owner: Ignacio Gutierrez
Club: Casuals | Location: Historic Arsenal, Benicia, California

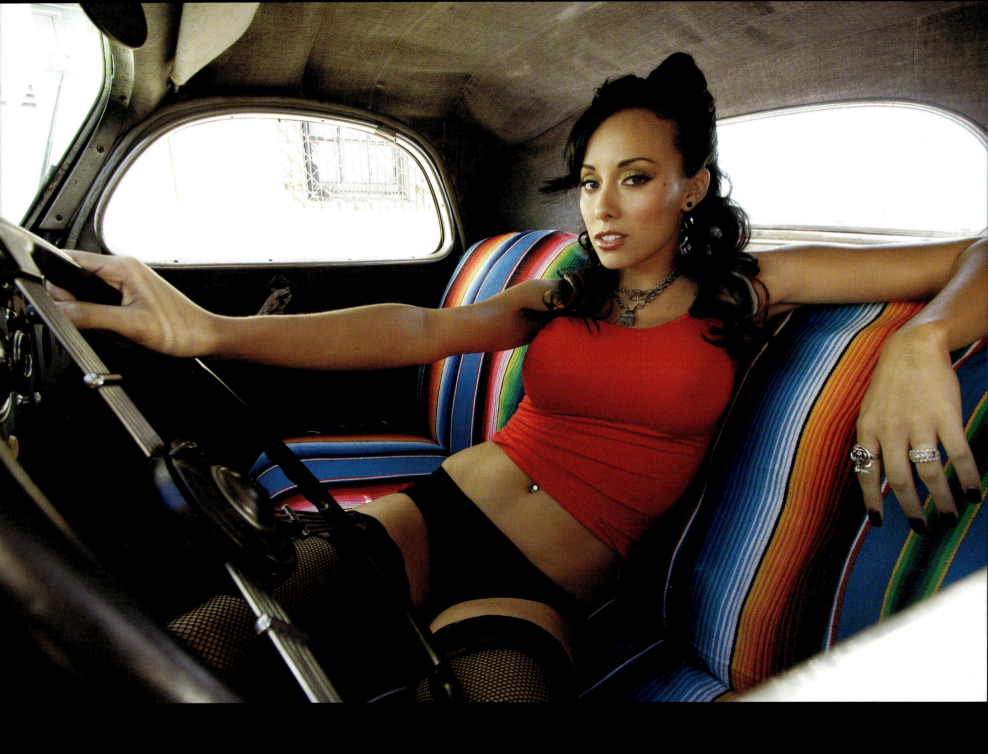

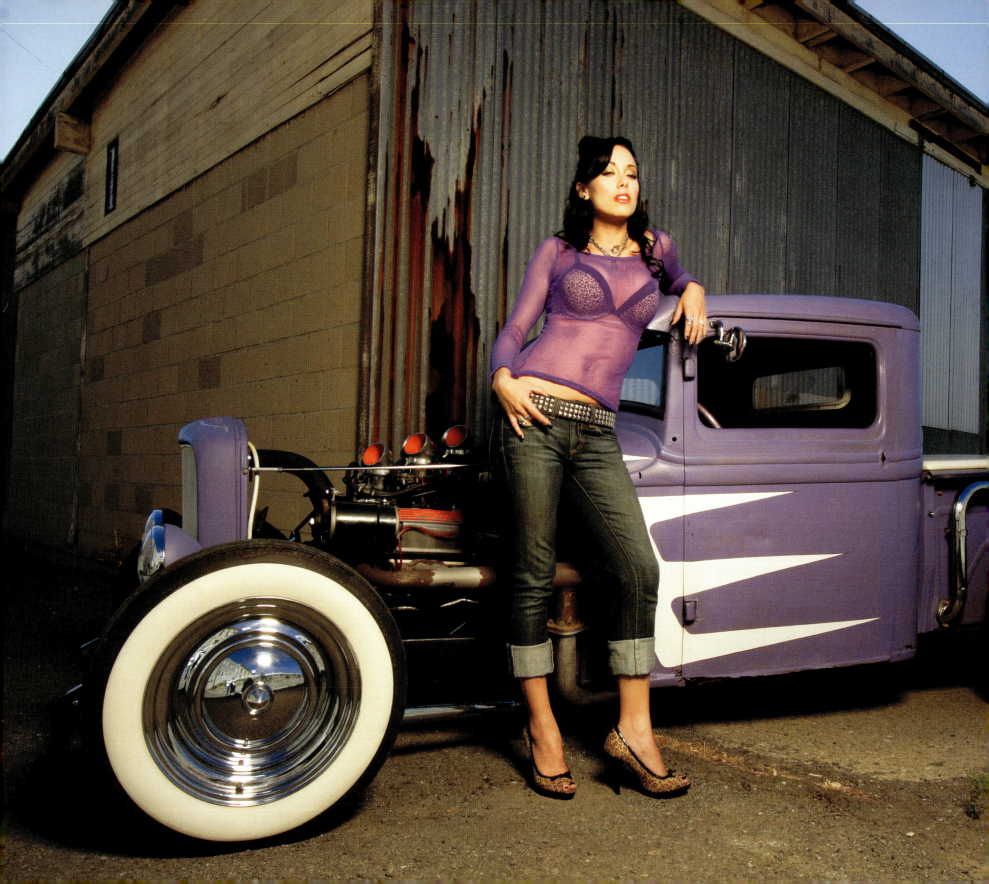

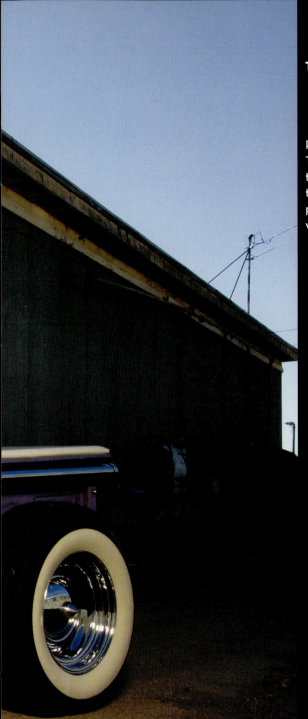

TERESA | 1932 Ford Pickup | Owner: Gunar Hansken | Club: Swanx | Location: Historic Arsenal, Benicia, California

Passionate in purple, Teresa makes the twenty years it took to get Gunar's Deuce pickup on the road well worth the wait.

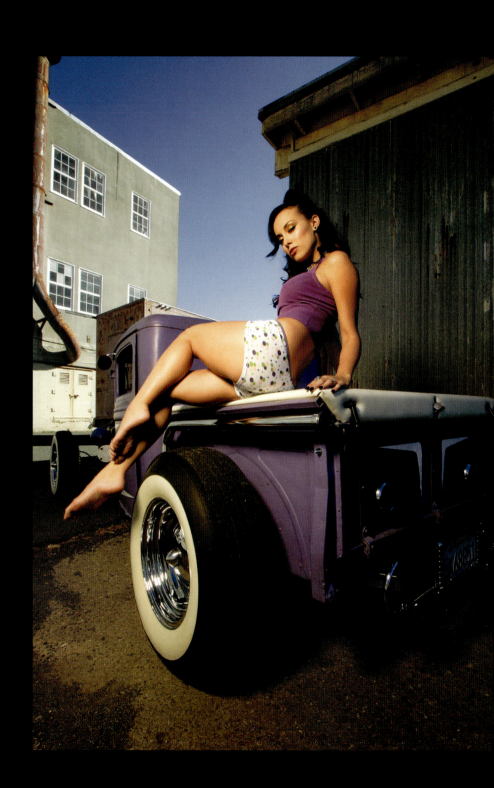

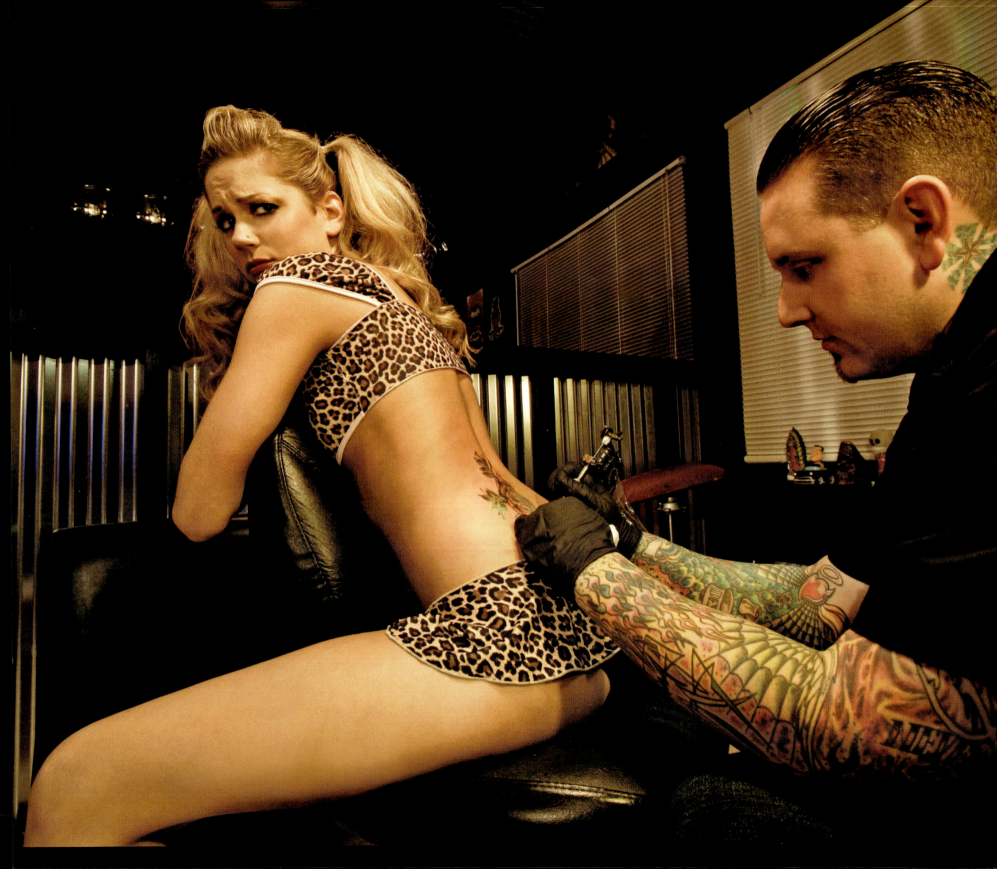

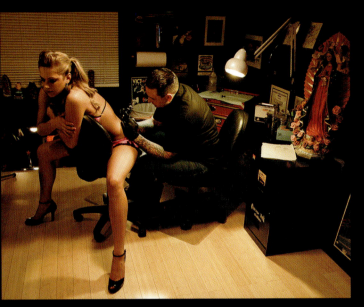

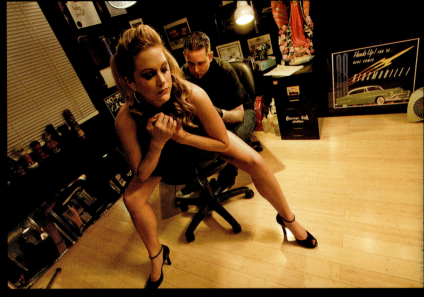

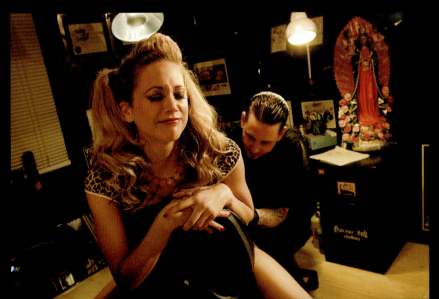

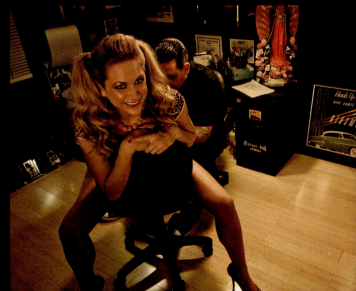

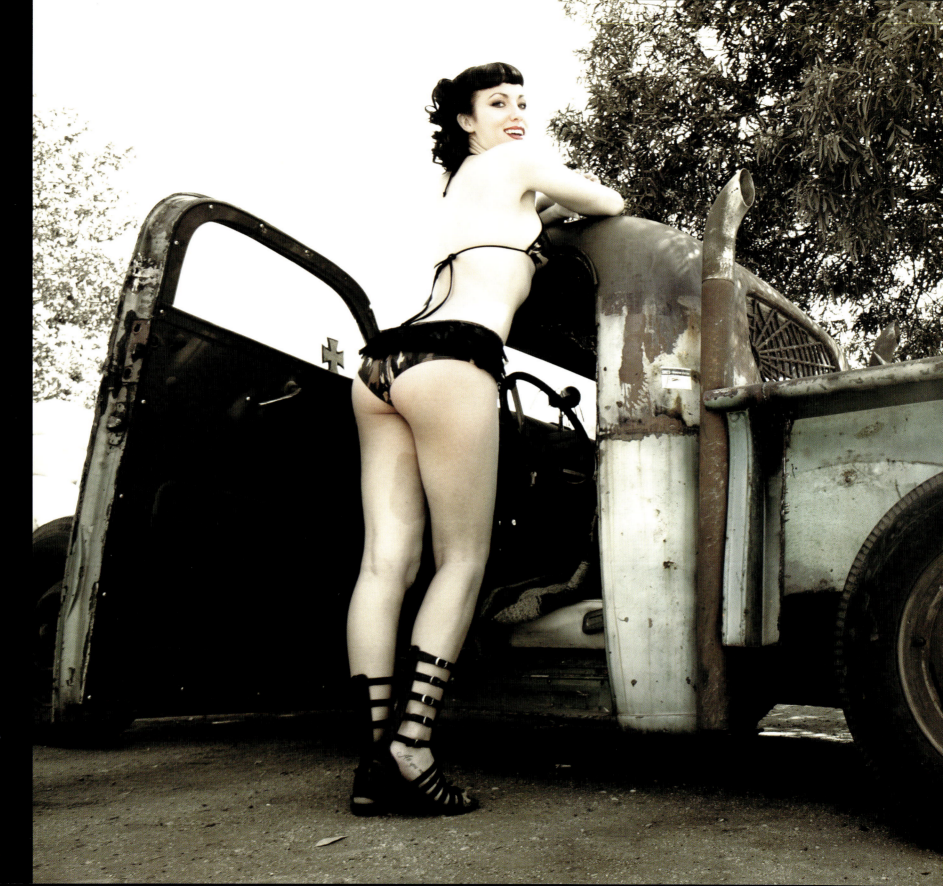

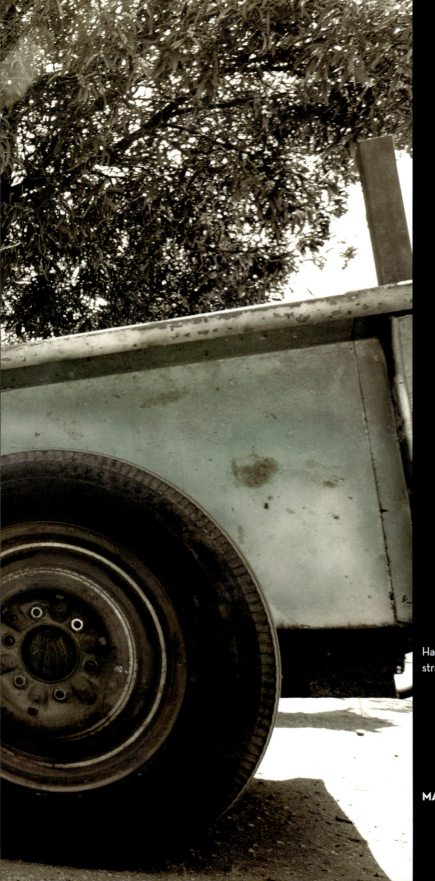

Have you not been entertained? Marlena looks the part of hot roddin' gladiator with her camo bikini and strap-alicious footware worthy of kickin' up dust on the Colosseum floor.

MARLENA | 1941 Chevy Pickup | Owner: Gerry Taylor | Location: Fomoso Drags, Bakersfield, California

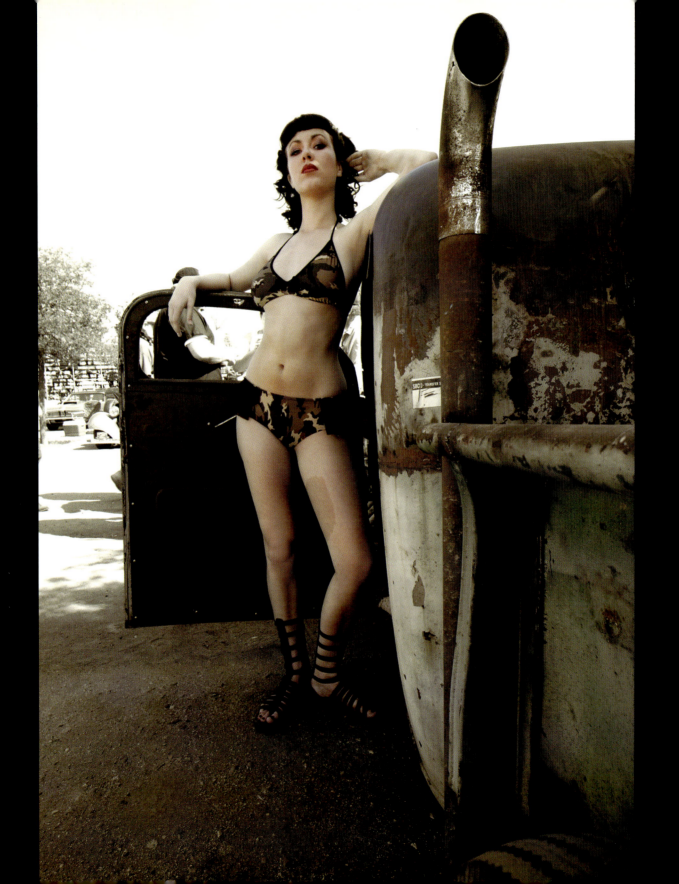

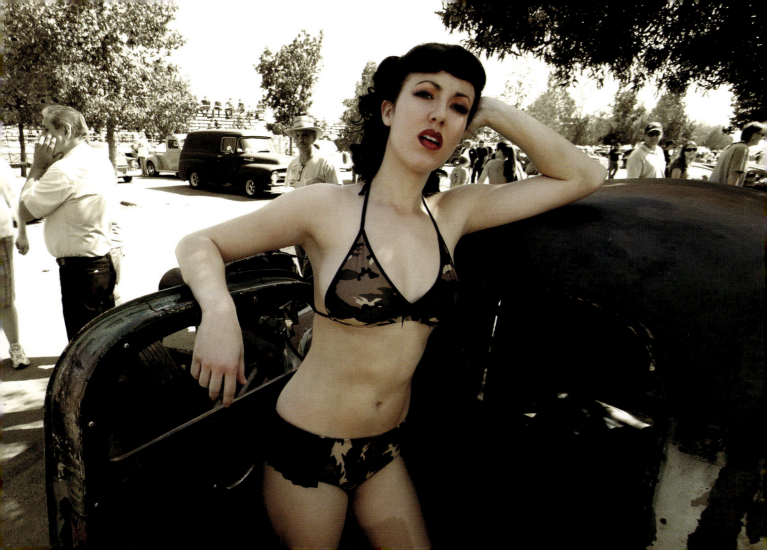

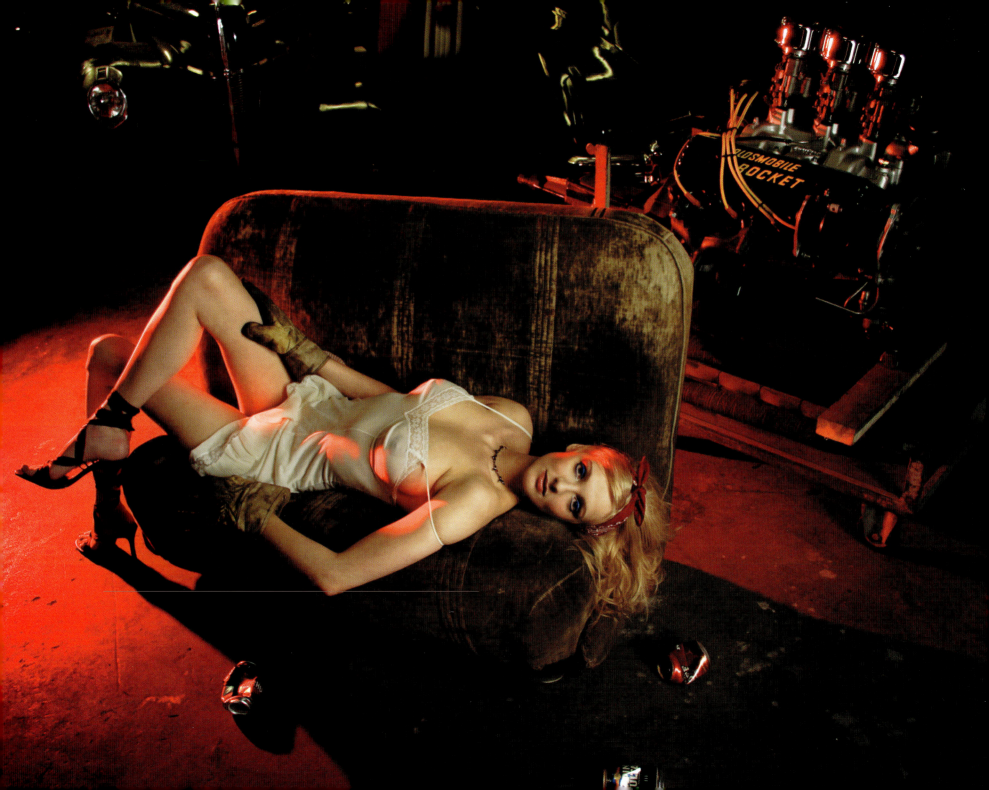

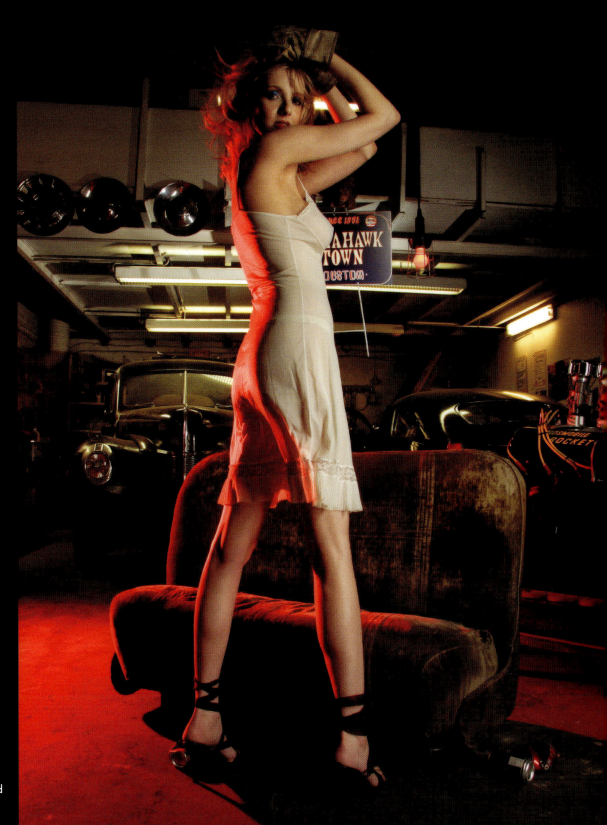

PIA | Owner: Lexa Hakkarainen | Club: Tomahawk Town | Location: Helsinki, Finland

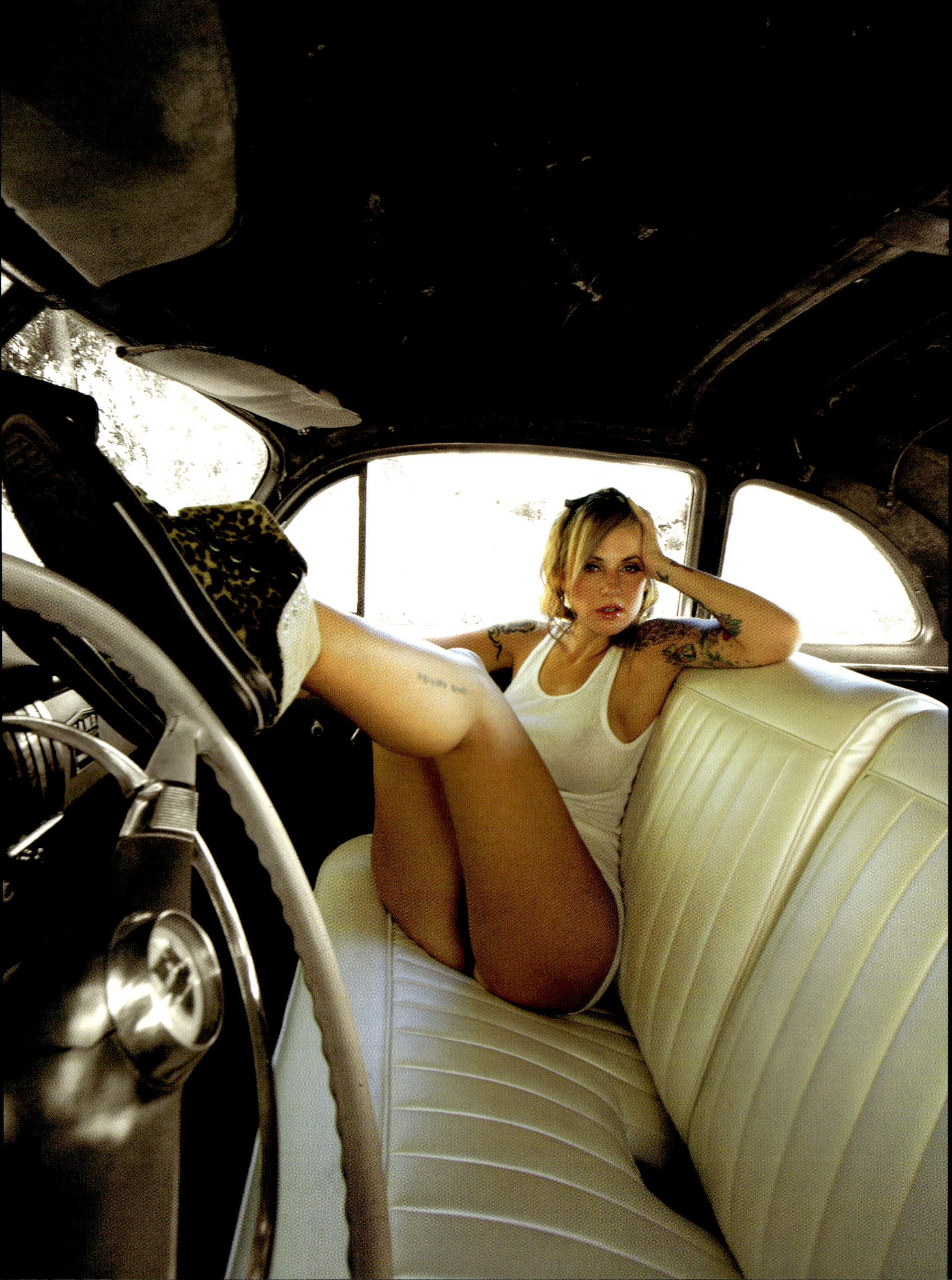

NIKKI | 1951 Chevy Coupe | Owner: Bryan Rusk
Club: Villains | Location: Auburn, California

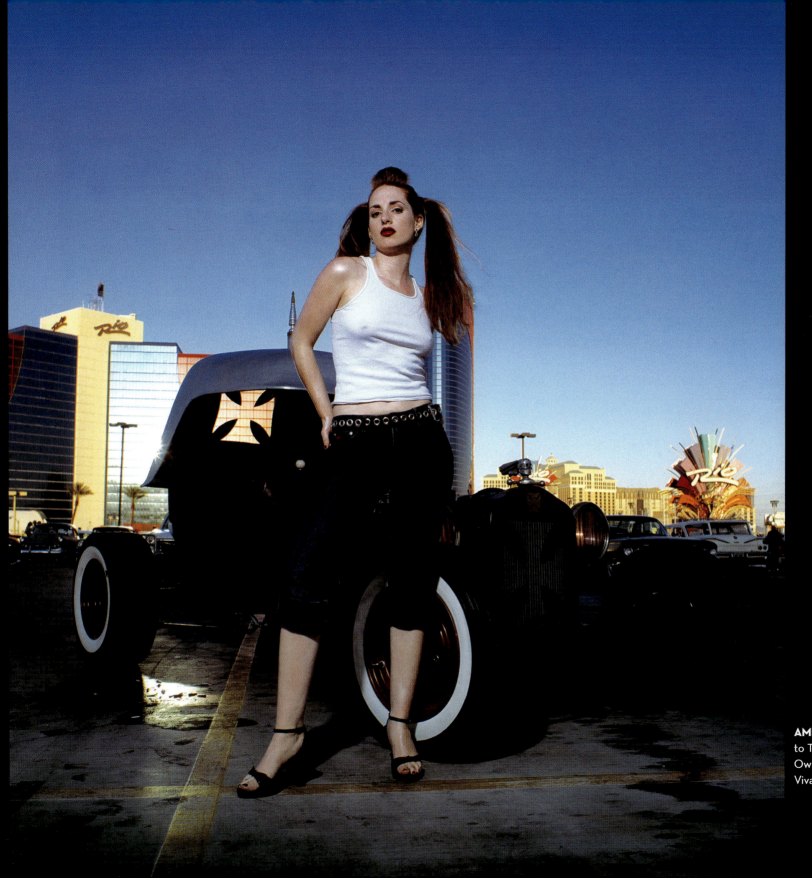

AMBER | *Von Zipper* tribute to Tom Daniel's *Red Baron* Owner: Guido | Location: Viva Las Vegas, Nevada

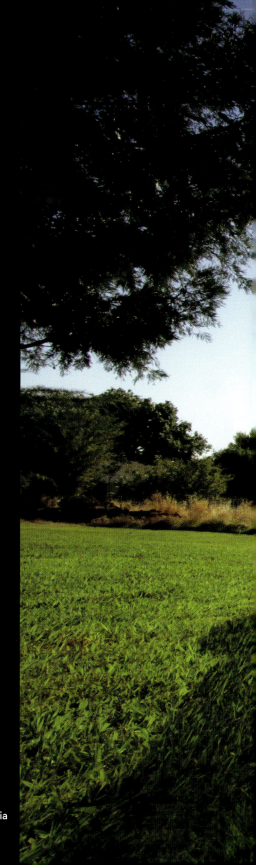

NIKKI | 1930 Ford Model A | Owner: Jim Luke | Club: Drag Lynx | Location: Auburn, California

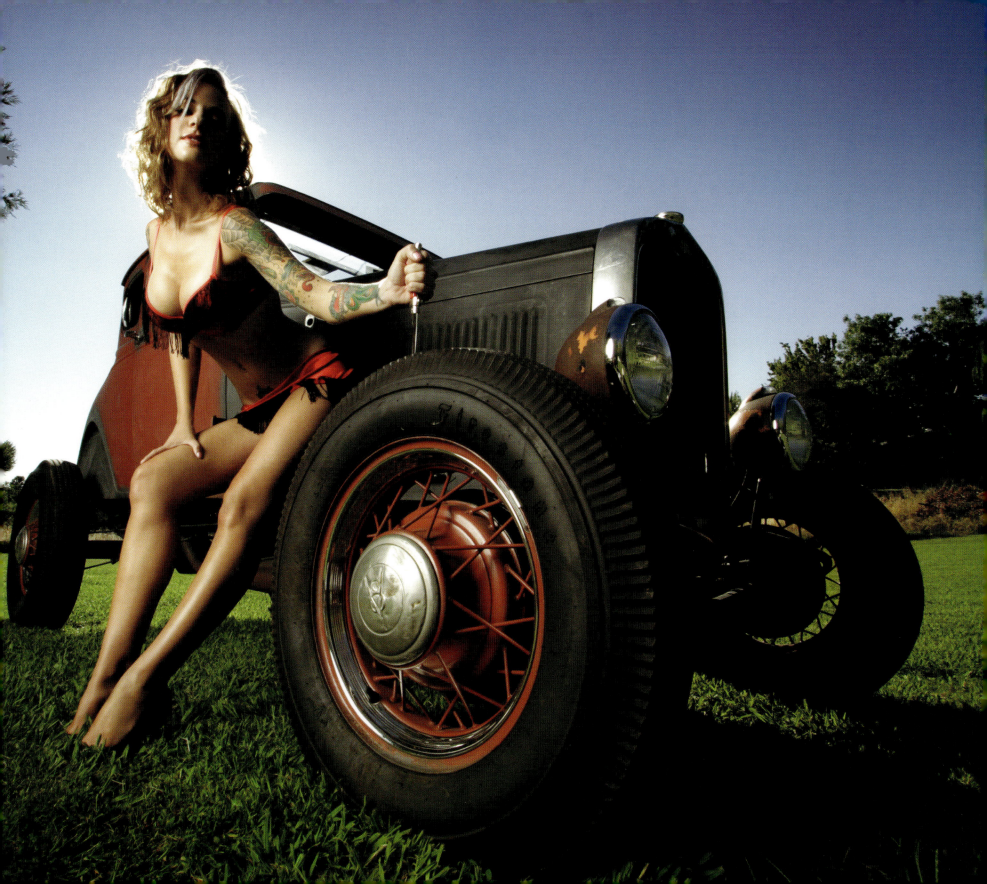

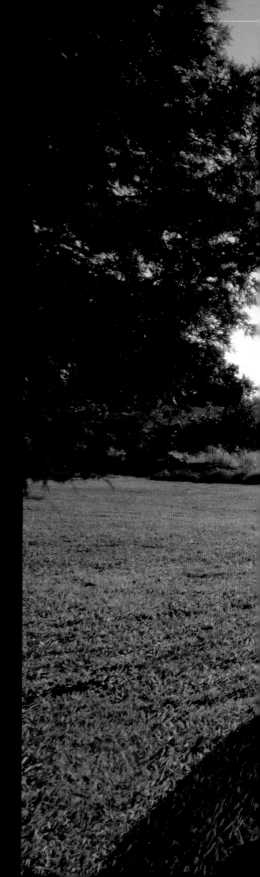

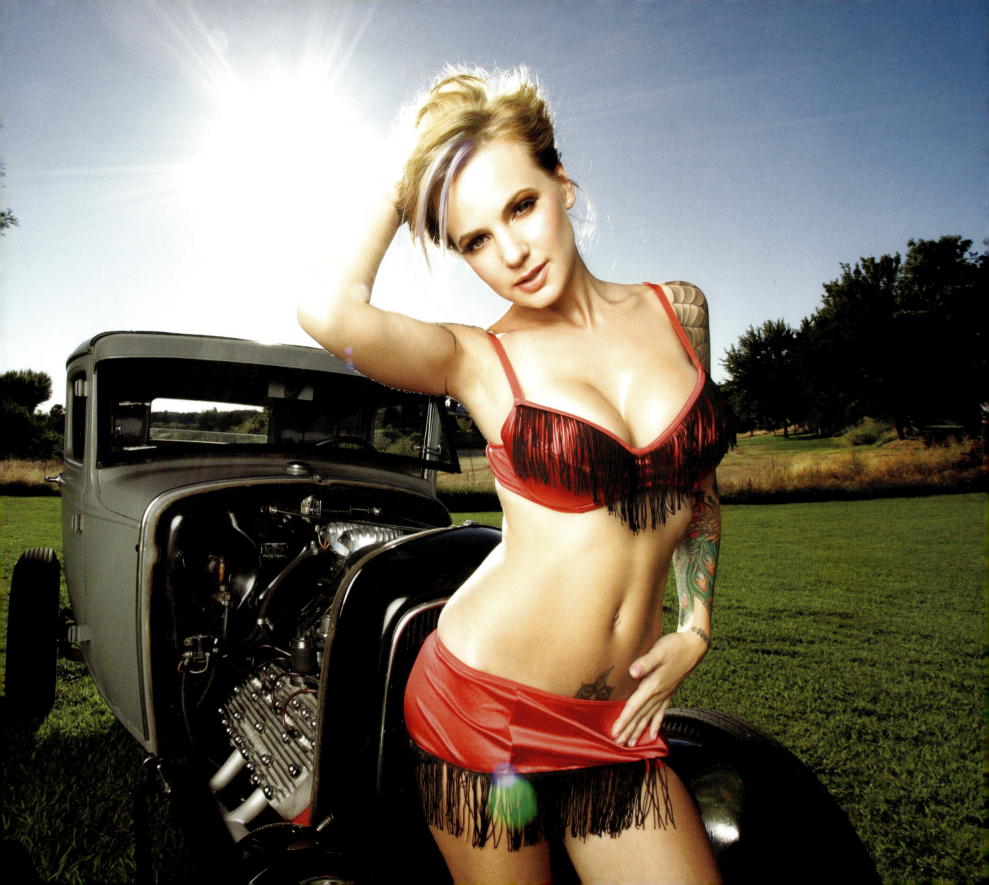

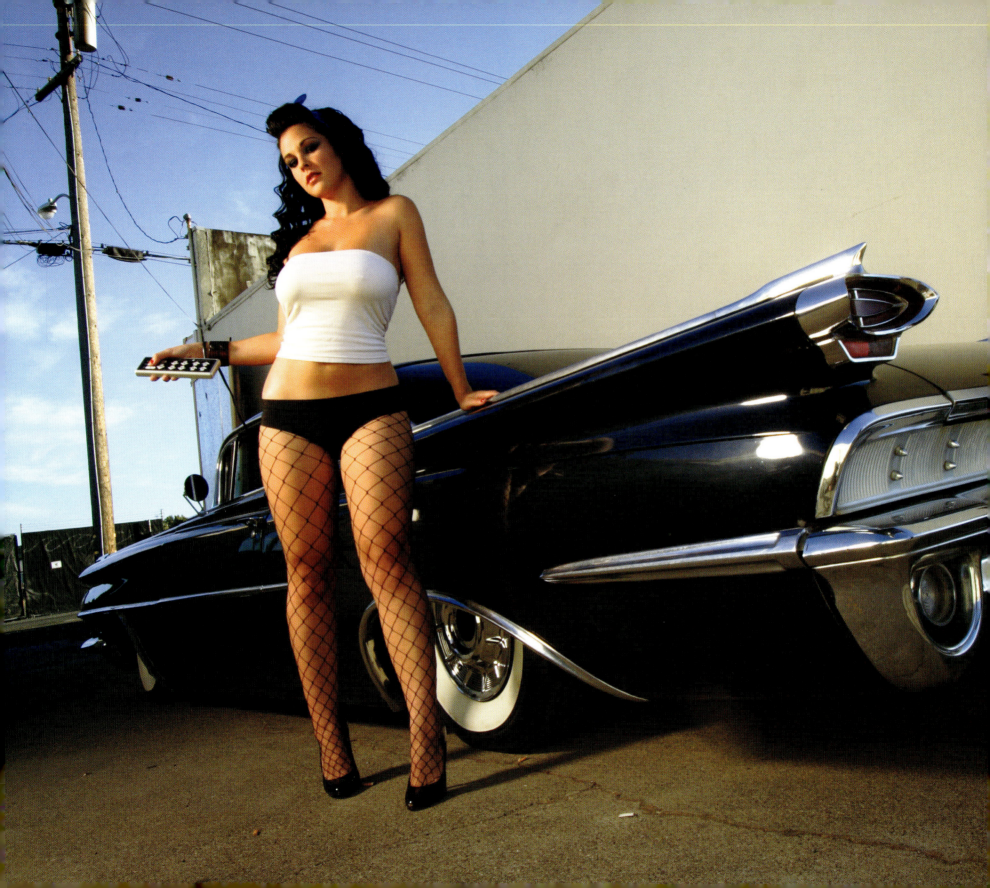

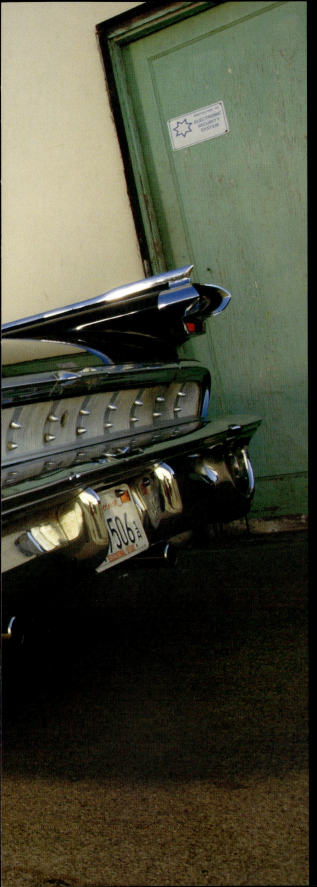

Lowridin' Laila enjoys being a control freak with Eric's Rocket at Seret Customs in V-town.

As Laila licked her lollipop while laying in Eric's Rocket 98, she had the Lemon Street gang trippin' over one another's tongues.

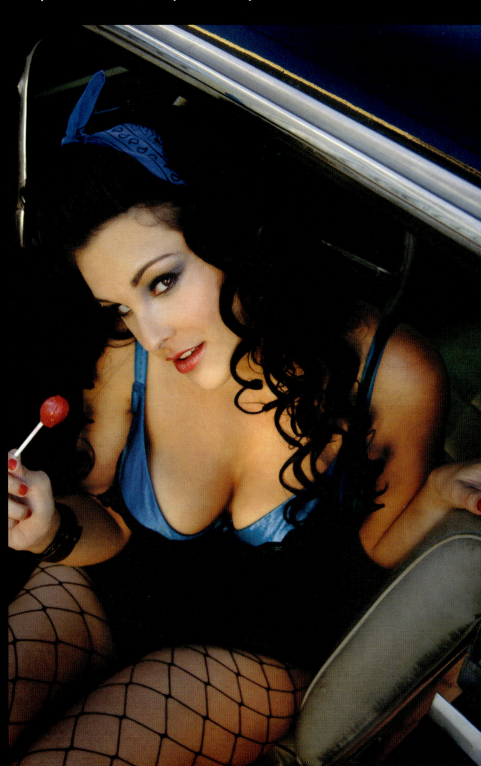

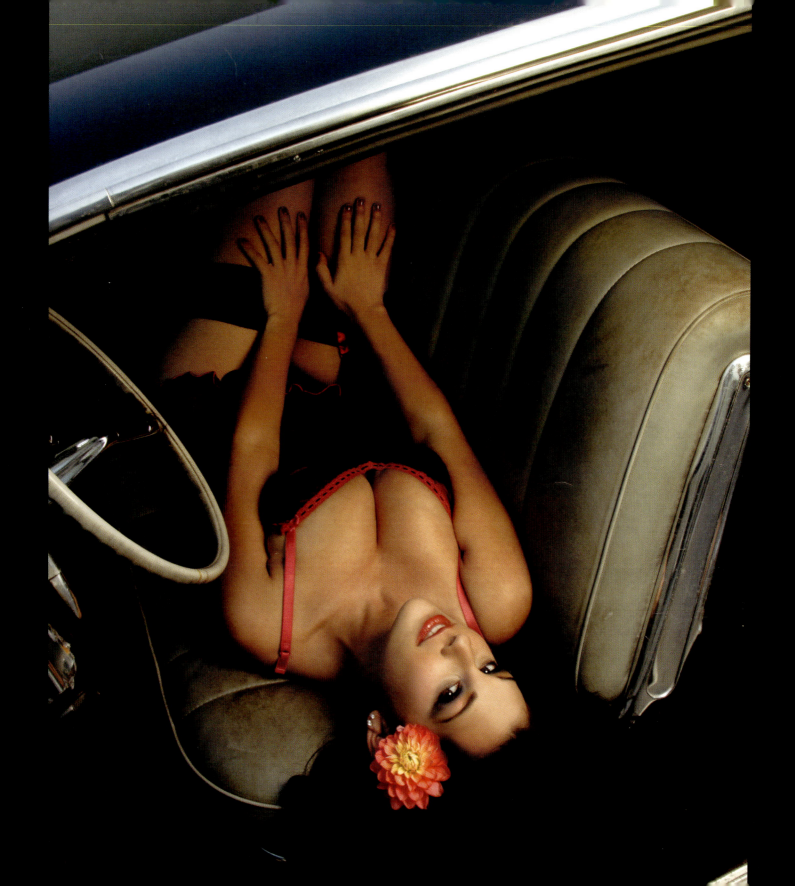

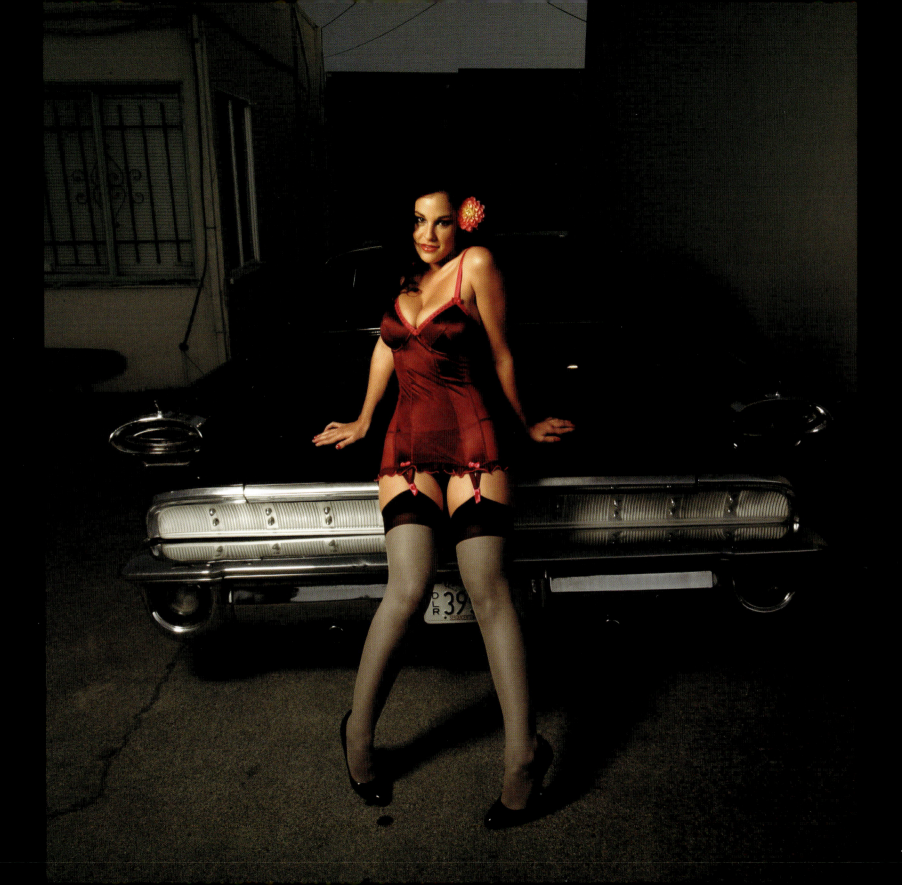

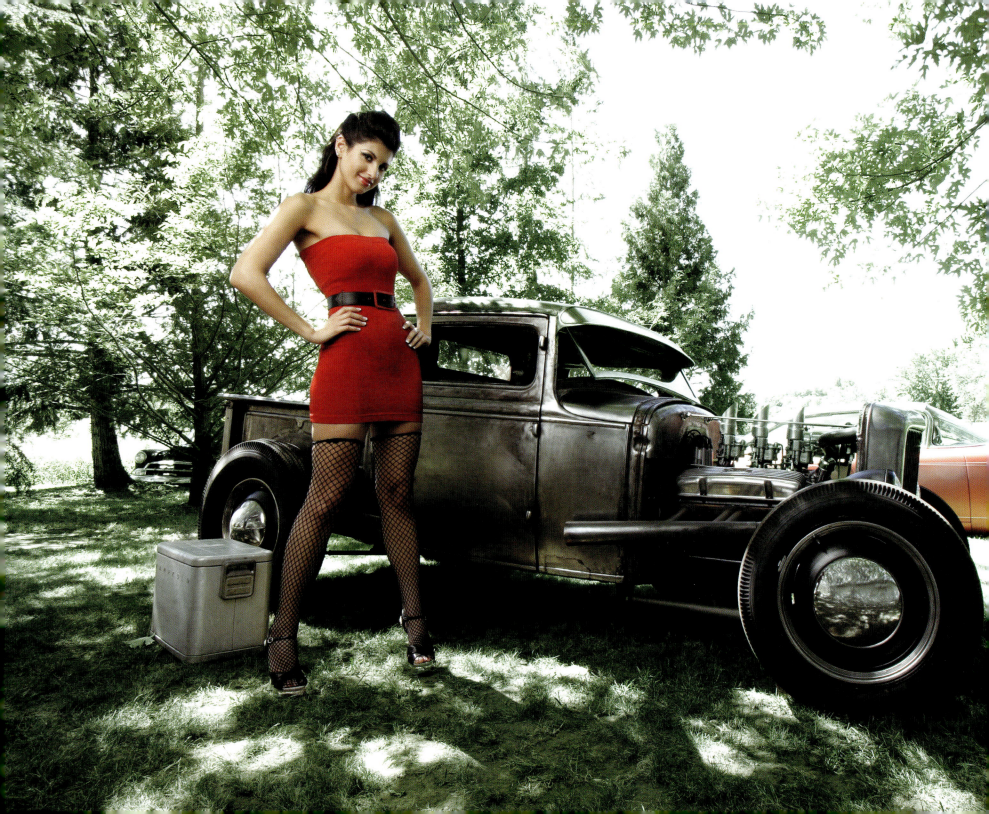

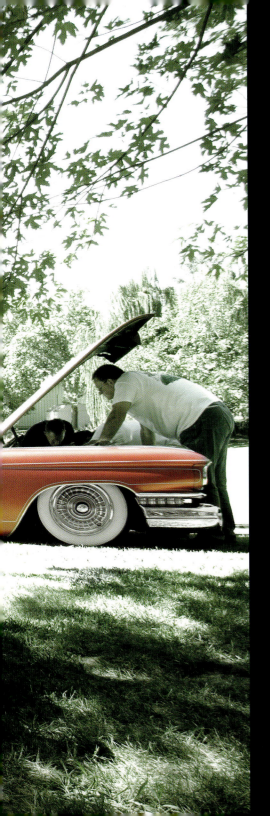

JAMIE | 1930 Ford Pickup | Owner: Pete Cannarozzi | Location: Auburn, California

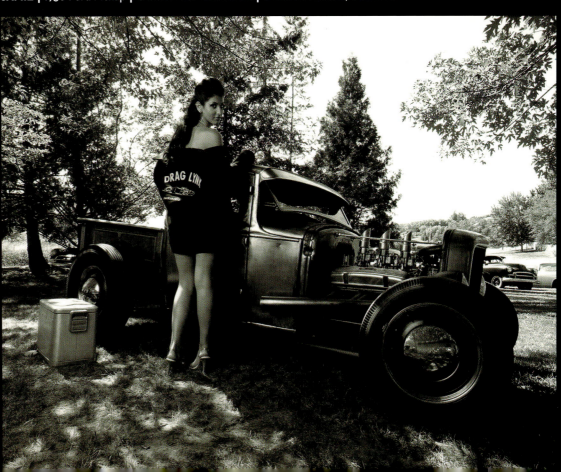

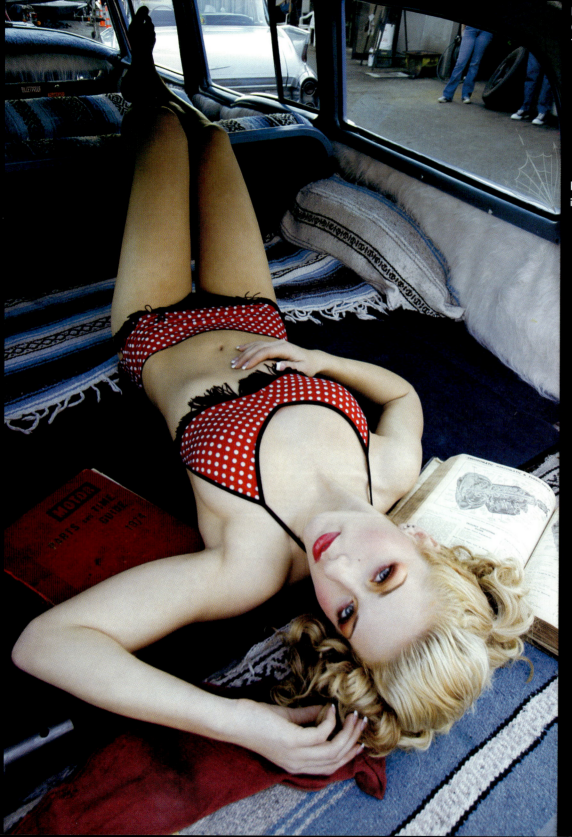

HALEY | 1956 Buick Wagon with Nailhead
Owner: Brent Wilson **|** Location: The Used
Tire Shop, Vacaville, California

Haley brushes up on Pontiac engine specs
in the back seat of Brent's Buick.

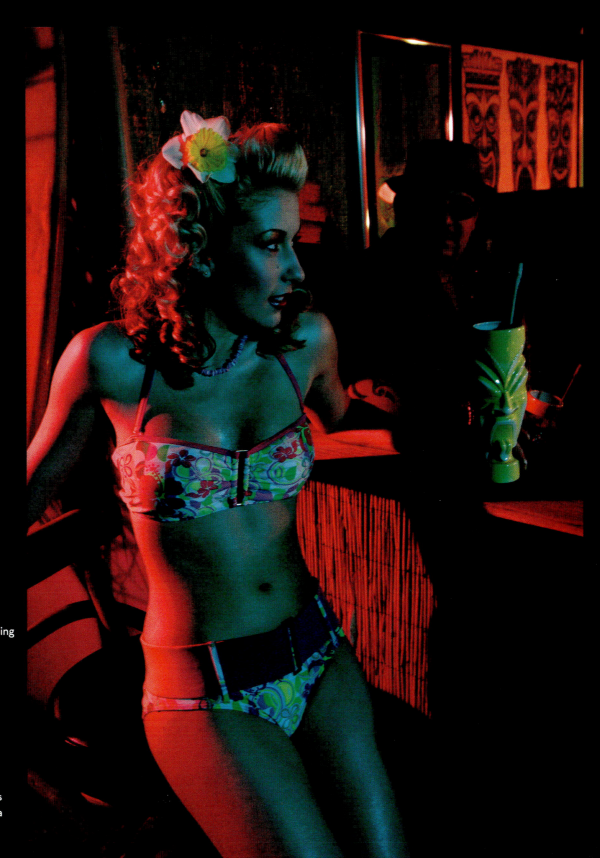

Hula-hipped Haley enjoys a refreshing Mai Tai inside the club's tiki hut.

HALEY | Location: Boris Hickman's "Hickman Hut," Vacaville, California

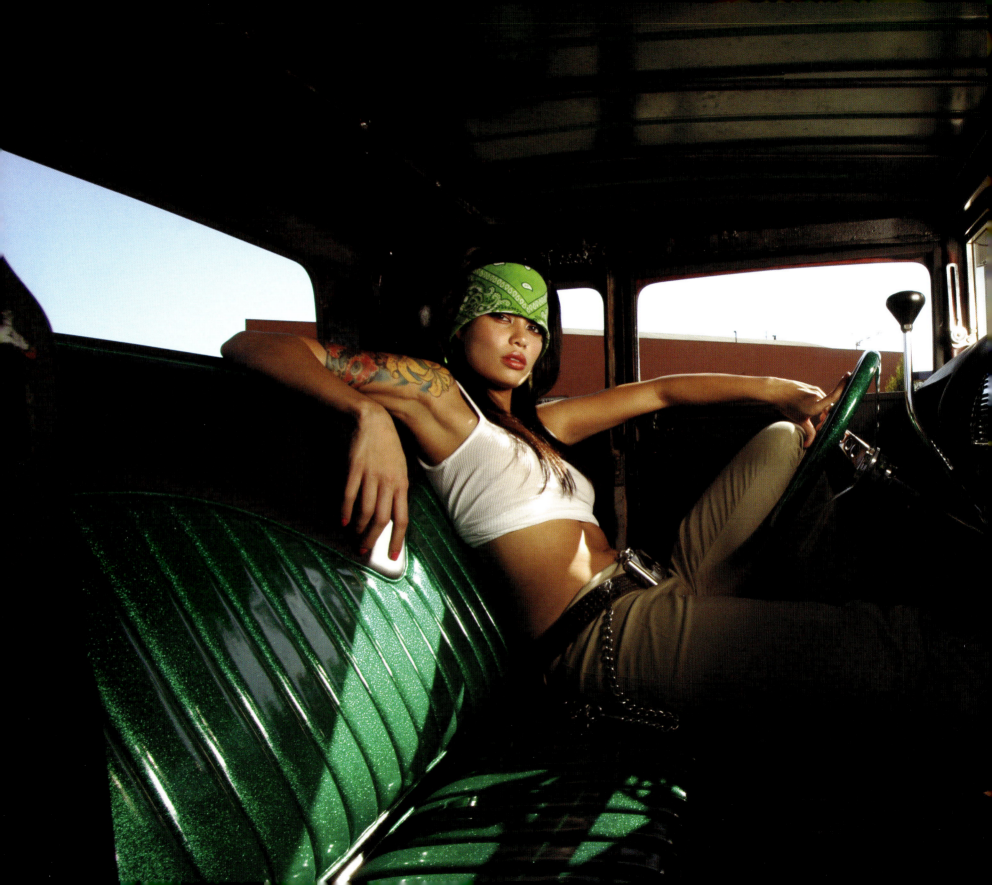

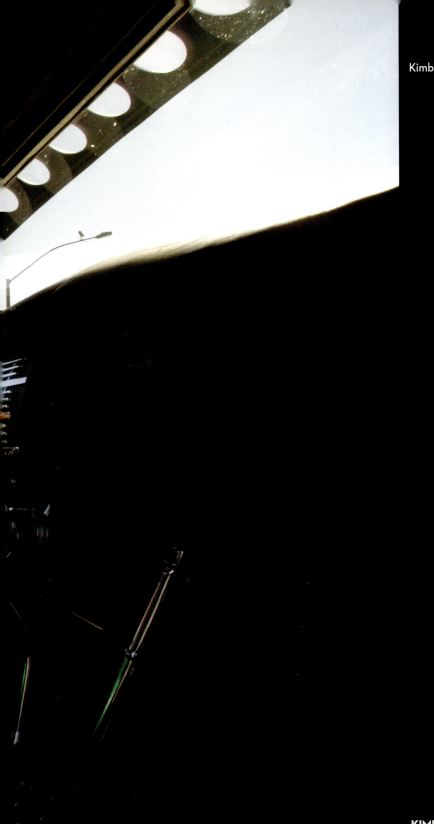

Kimberly warms the metalflake seats while swatting glances.

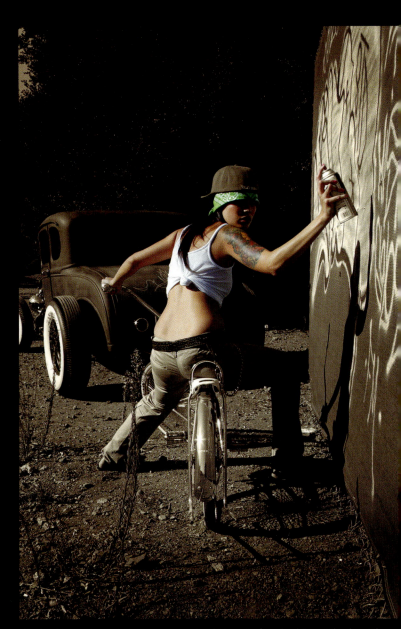

Cholita Kimberly embellishes the walls of Napa before bad boy Gil, a.k.a. "the redheaded Mexican," bails her out.

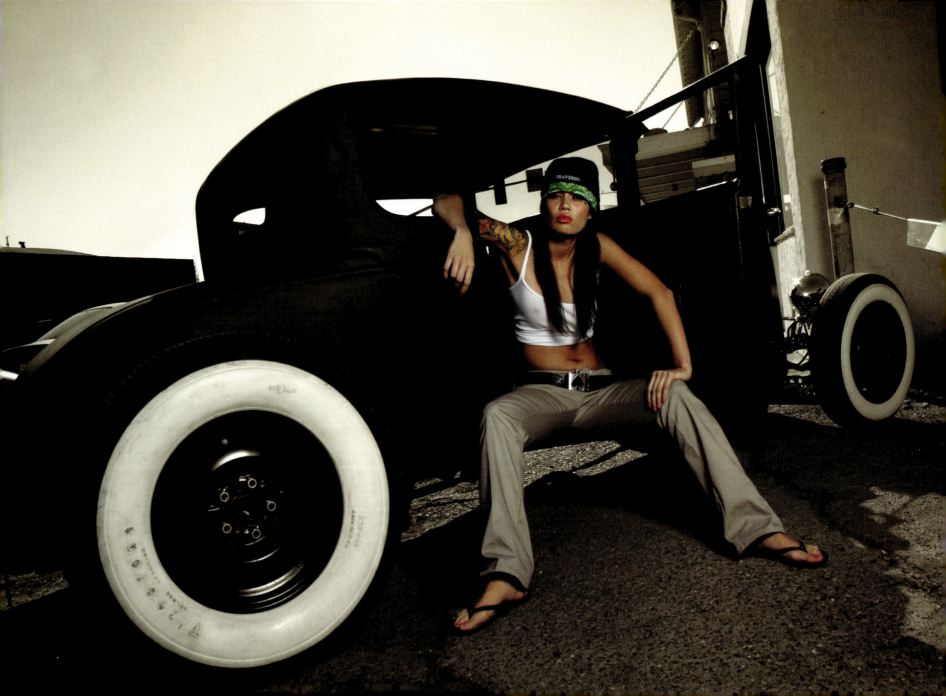

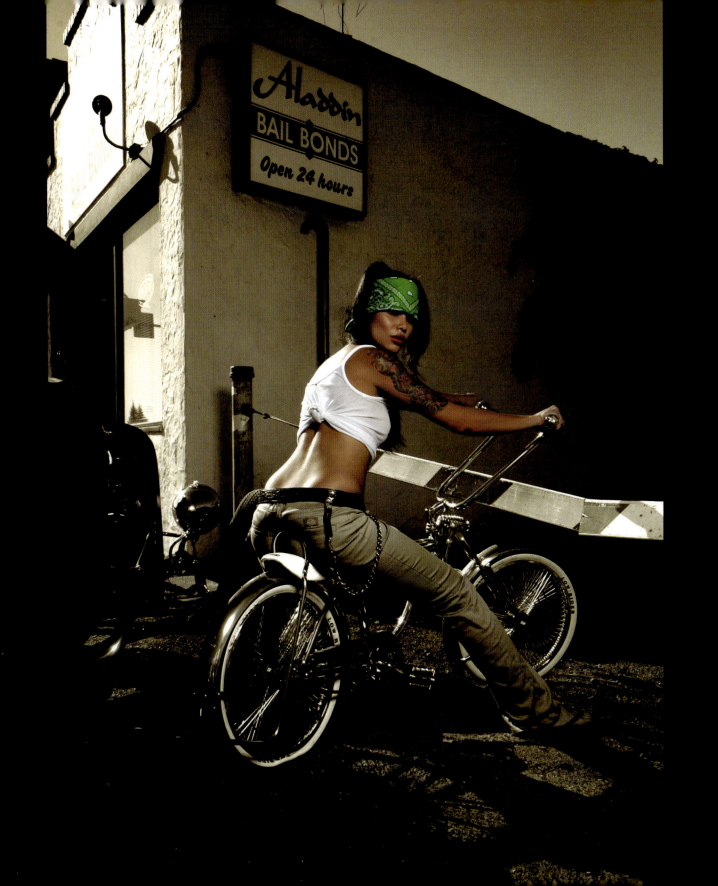

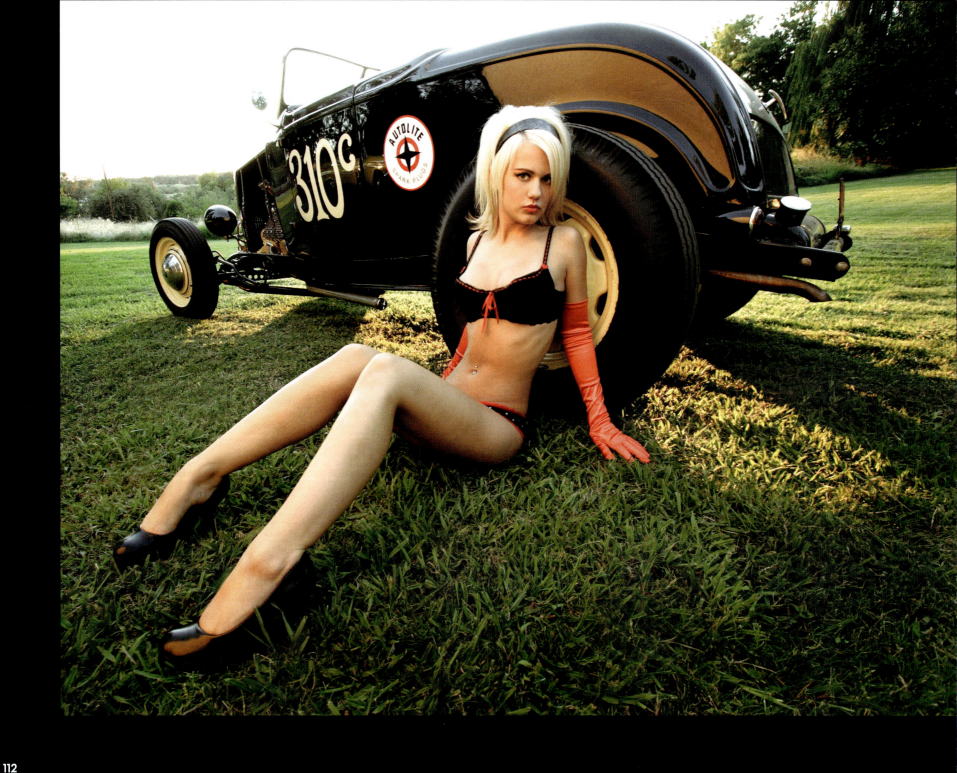

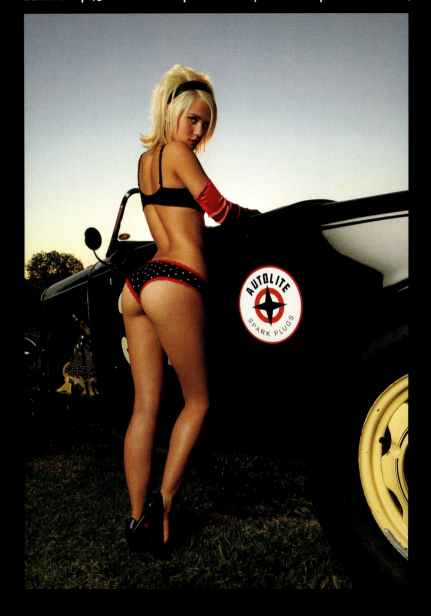

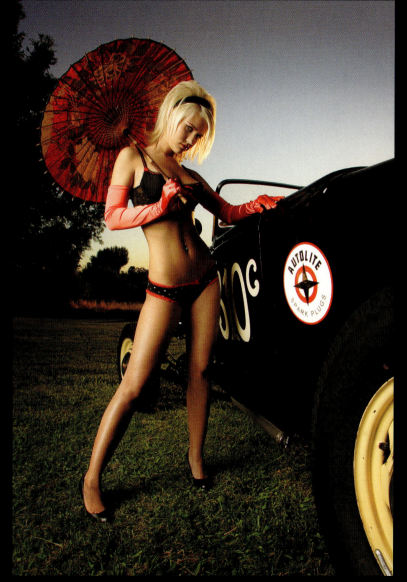

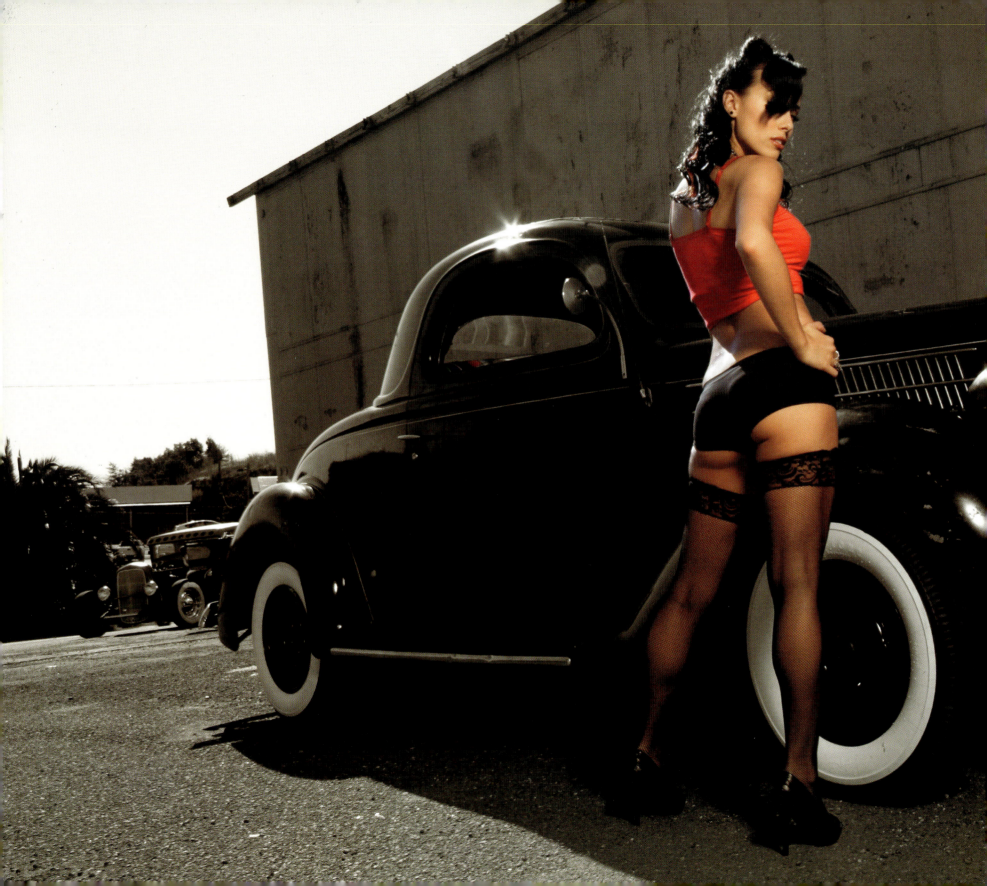

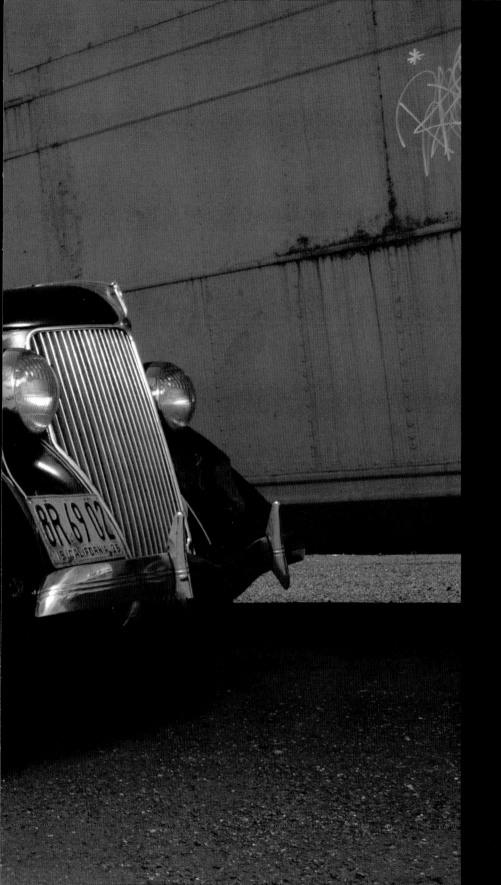

custom cuties

The new *Mercury* four-door pulled on to the side of the highway and stopped. The whisper of its motor was smooth and factory-soft. Nervously, the youth at the wheel turned and looked over his shoulder into the emptiness of the night. He sighed, dimmed the lights and flipped on the radio.

". . . and that's the headlines at three A.M. on Saturday morning. Fifty-five minutes from now we'll be back again with . . ."

Up ahead, the three-lane highway looked like twin ribbons of white candy in the moonlight. It looked that way because the center lane was asphalt, rough asphalt that seldom got slippery even in the winter. Some said the road had been built that way because black topping was cheaper than cement. Some said it had been so designed for added safety. No one, of course, really knew. It was just five miles of highway that stretched as straight as a yardstick through the valley north of Millville, population 7,280.

". . . a request for Judy Lane, singing, *I've Got My Love To Keep Me Warm* . . ."

A pair of headlights, moving rapidly, bore down upon the parked Mercury. The music rose and then, quite suddenly, died. Only the sounds of the pulsing motor and the rap of twin *Hollywoods* of the approaching car broke the stillness.

The *Ford*, a fifty-four model, pulled alongside the *Mercury* and halted. Its rear, the length of the two-door accentuated by the full continental tire kit, was low and it hugged the ground. The idle of the *Ford* was rough and unsteady and the continuous rumble from the straight-through mufflers drowned out all sounds from the *Mercury*.

The driver of the *Ford* leaned across the passenger in the front seat and rolled down the window.

"You still want to try it, Freddie?" It was a girl's voice; a low voice and slightly contemptuous. A cigarette glowed in the shadows and she laughed. "I told you, I can lay rubber on the road with this thing at sixty." She laughed again. "You couldn't even pass a washing machine at sixty, Freddie."

The young man in the Mercury ignored her remark. "Only one thing," he said. "You sure the troopers are off the road now?"

"They eat between three and four," the girl replied. "At one of the diners in town. We always drag out here when they're down there." The girl's tone was now sardonic, impatient. "You going to chicken out, Freddie?"

The girl jammed her foot against the gas pedal, lifted it; the *Hollywoods* bellowed and belched power. A train whistle screeched in the distance. The challenge of the road lay before them.

"I ain't chicken," the boy retorted. "I just wanted to make sure, that's all. You know what they'd say if the son of the county judge—"

The girl settled herself behind the wheel and the *Hollywoods* roared. The car rocked, steadied and then rocked again.

"Lay to it!" she shouted.

The boy fed fuel to the *Mercury* and shot out into the right lane. Swiftly, with the staccato drive of a prizefighter's punches, the *Mercury* changed gears.

"Sucker," the girl breathed.

The *Ford* was a straight-stick and she took it away in second. The motor screamed, reached its peak and at seventy she snapped it into high. Seconds later she threw it into overdrive and the *Ford* began to devour the vacant highway the way a hungry cow eats grass. The dual carbs sucked greedily at the air and gas and the tachometer on the steering column moved beyond the 4500 R.P.M. mark, wavered briefly and then continued its upward climb.

Less than a mile down the road the *Ford* shot past the *Mercury*, its tires rumbling on the rough macadam. The car swayed as it crossed the dividing line and moved over into the righthand lane.

Two miles beyond that, the lights of the *Mercury* were far behind.

At the end of the straightaway, five miles from the starting point, the *Ford* slowed quickly for a sharp curve. It rounded the curve and continued to decrease speed. As the lights of the town drew closer, the speed of the car dropped to a normal forty miles an hour.

"Nobody can touch this bomb," the girl said to her companion.

When she reached the entrance of a huge gravel bank the girl braked the car and swung the two-door off the road. She made a complete circle, barely missing a deep hole filled with muddy water and brought the *Ford* to a stop. She dimmed the lights and cut the ignition switch. Except for the gurgling sounds that throbbed in the radiator, the night was quiet.

"Wise guy," the girl said. Her voice neither condemned the driver of the *Mercury* nor did it pity him. She relaxed against the cushion and lit a cigarette. "When will they ever learn that a good old car is better than anything new and stock?"

The glow of the match reflected the pleasure in her eyes, although she could find little satisfaction in having beaten Freddie Craver. So many people had beaten Freddie at so many things that the effort was almost routine. It was the *Ford*, however, that pleased her. It had it, it really did.

"Freddie must have gotten scared and started to walk," she said, watching the darkness of the highway.

Her passenger laughed nervously.

"I-I was scared, too. You were doing a hundred and fifteen when I stopped looking."

Jayne Barton filled her lungs with cigarette smoke and glanced at the girl beside her. She could feel her breasts rising and falling, the hard, tense thrust of the nipples shoving out against her bra.

"I'm sorry I frightened you," Jayne said reflectively. "I know you don't like to go fast, Ruthie—but what could I do? Freddie only came into *The Rest* because he saw the car outside and thought he'd find Eric. He's always wanted to beat Eric in a drag—who doesn't?—and I guess he figured his daddy's new *Merc* was the best bet. He ought to have known better. I couldn't even do it with the *Caddy*. So—well, he lost twenty-five bucks. So what? He'll turn around, drive back to the corners, sneak into town the back way and he'll never pay it, that's so what."

"You really think so, Jayne?"

The driver of the *Ford* opened the window and snapped the cigarette to the ground.

"If Freddie ever wasted twenty-five dollars that way, his old man would give him thirty days on the county," she said.

Lights moved down the highway but it was a truck. The truck went past, lumbering, and the night closed in around them.

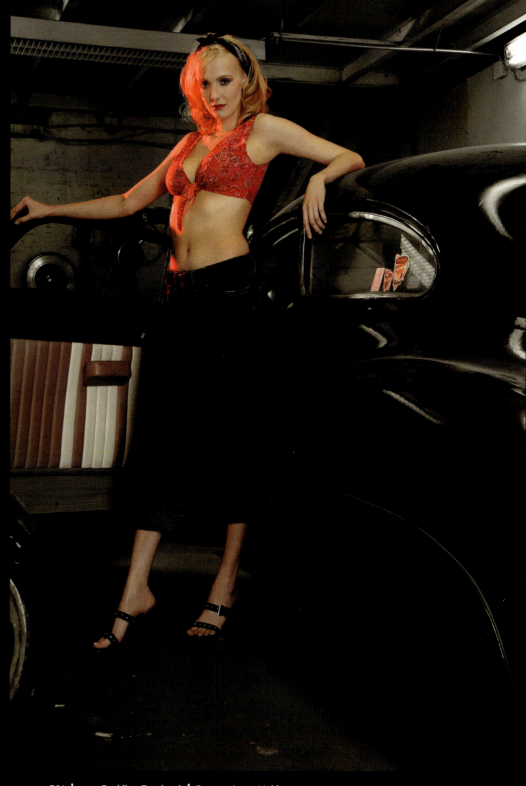

PIA | 1942 Cadillac Fastback | Owner: Lexa Hakkarainen
Club: Tomahawk Town | Location: Helsinki, Finland

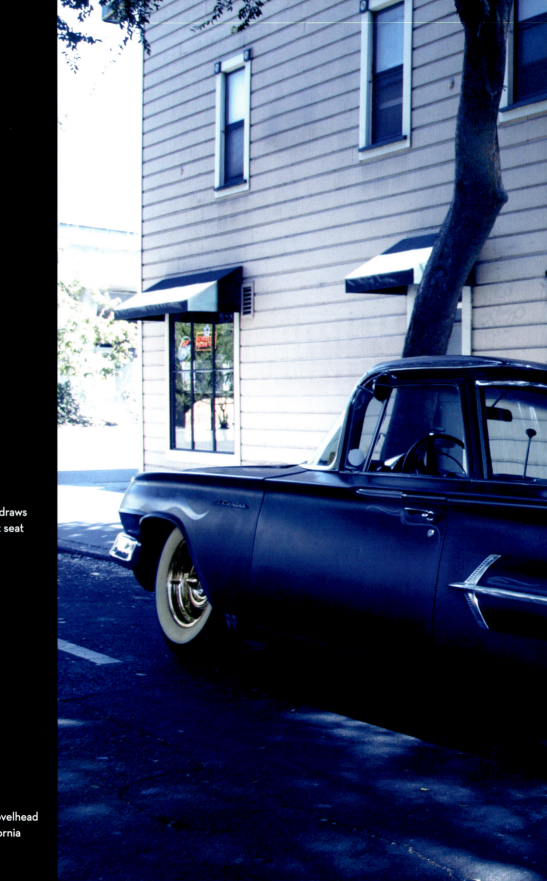

Loitering at the liquor store in her itsy-bitsy blue bikini, Ashley draws quite a crowd, but she doesn't mind as she cozies up to the hot seat of Slim's shovelhead.

ASHLEY | 1960 Chevy El Camino & 1969 Harley Davidson Shovelhead
Owner: Pete "Slim" Femenia **|** Location: Point Richmond, California

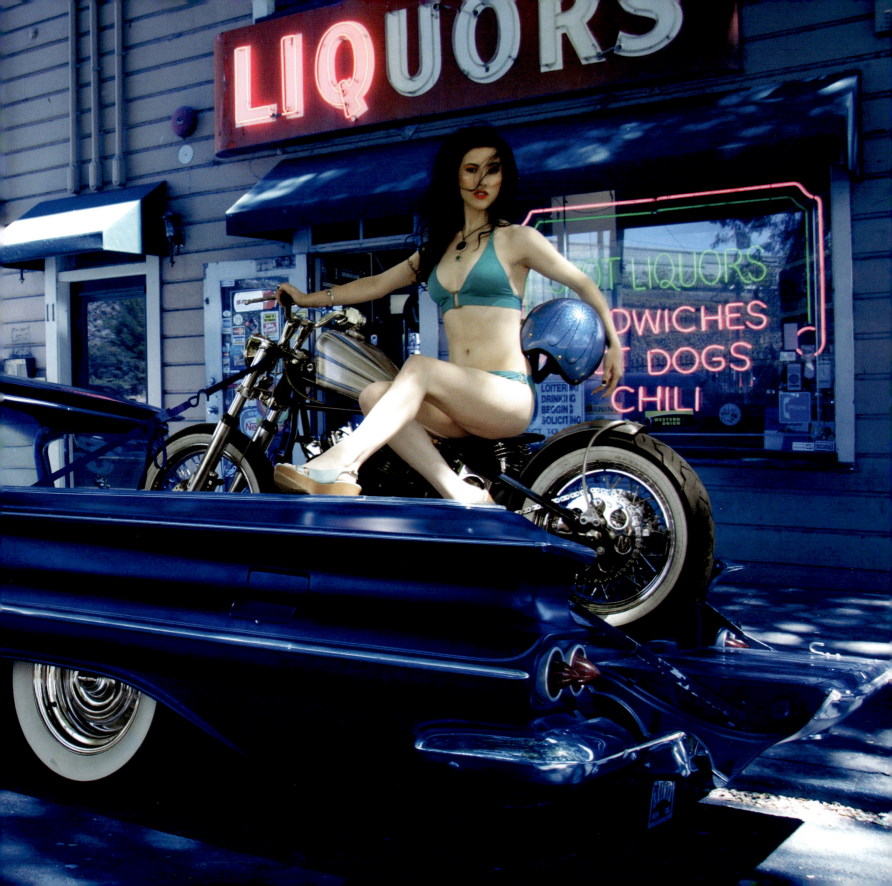

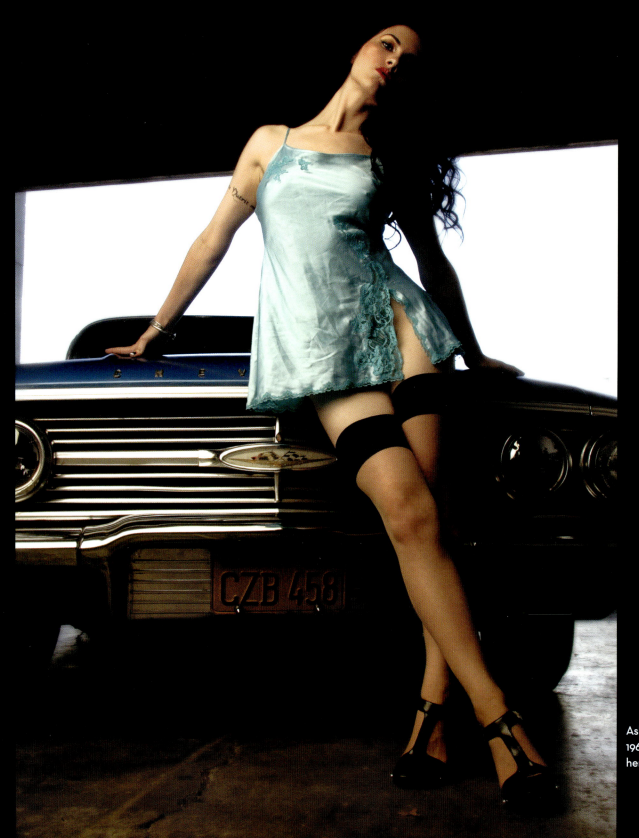

Ashley strokes the warm hood of Slim's 1960 El Camino custom while wearing her silk slip and full-fashion stockings.

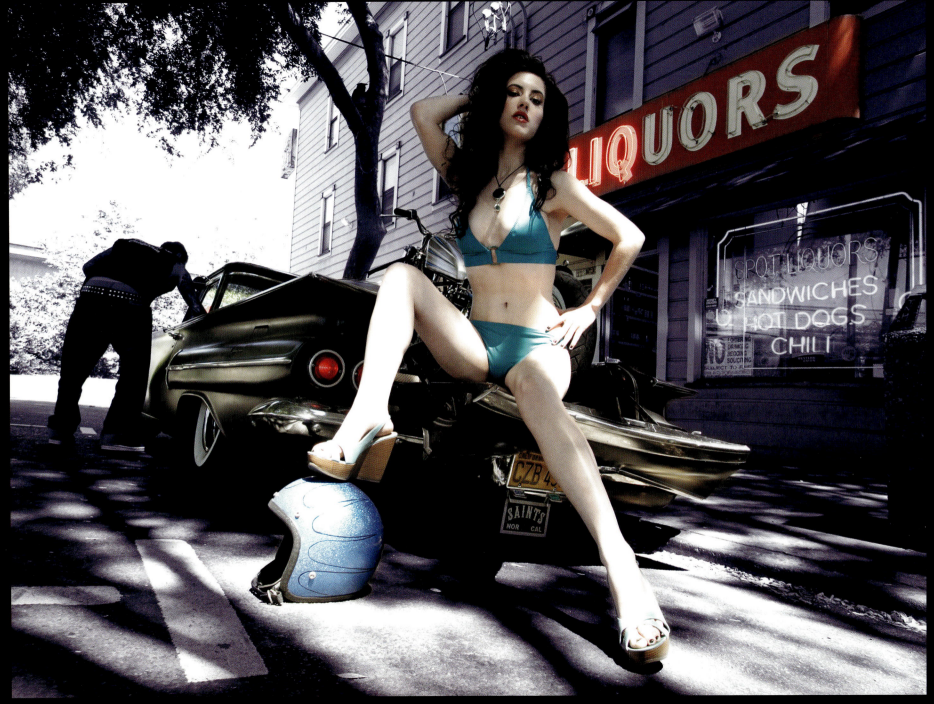

Ashley enjoys the cool breeze on her alabaster skin as she tosses her raven hair and shows what she thinks of the helmet law.

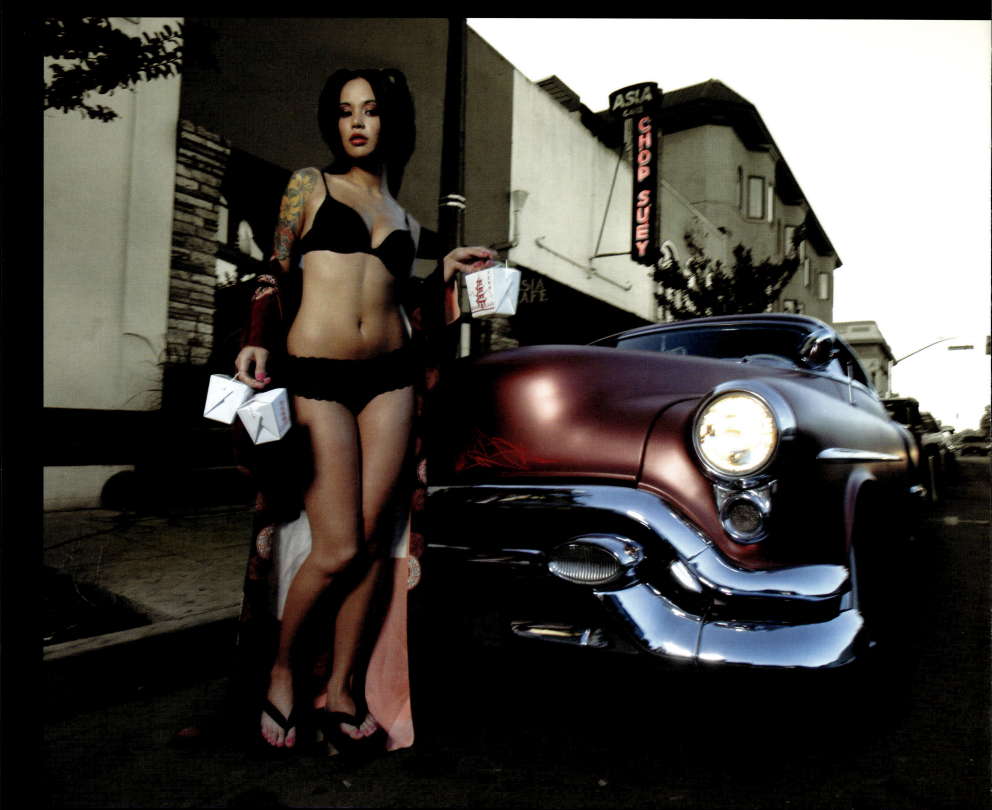

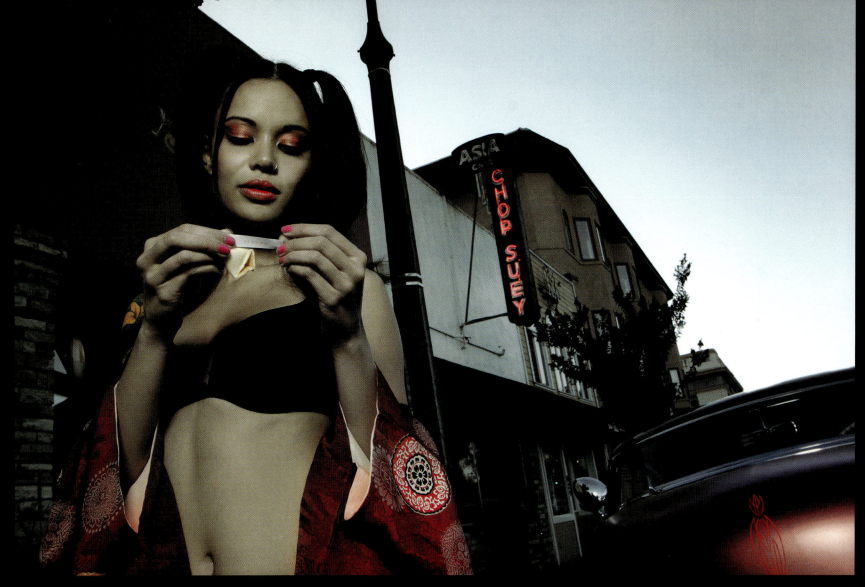

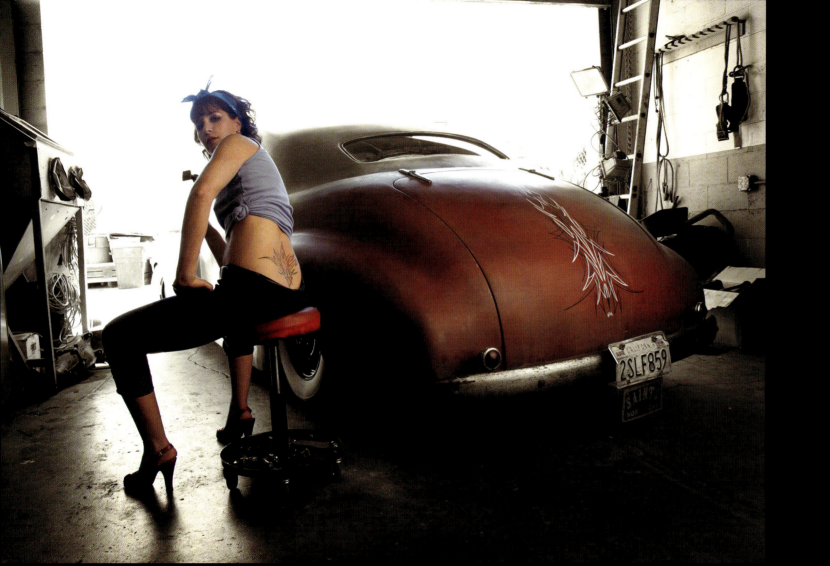

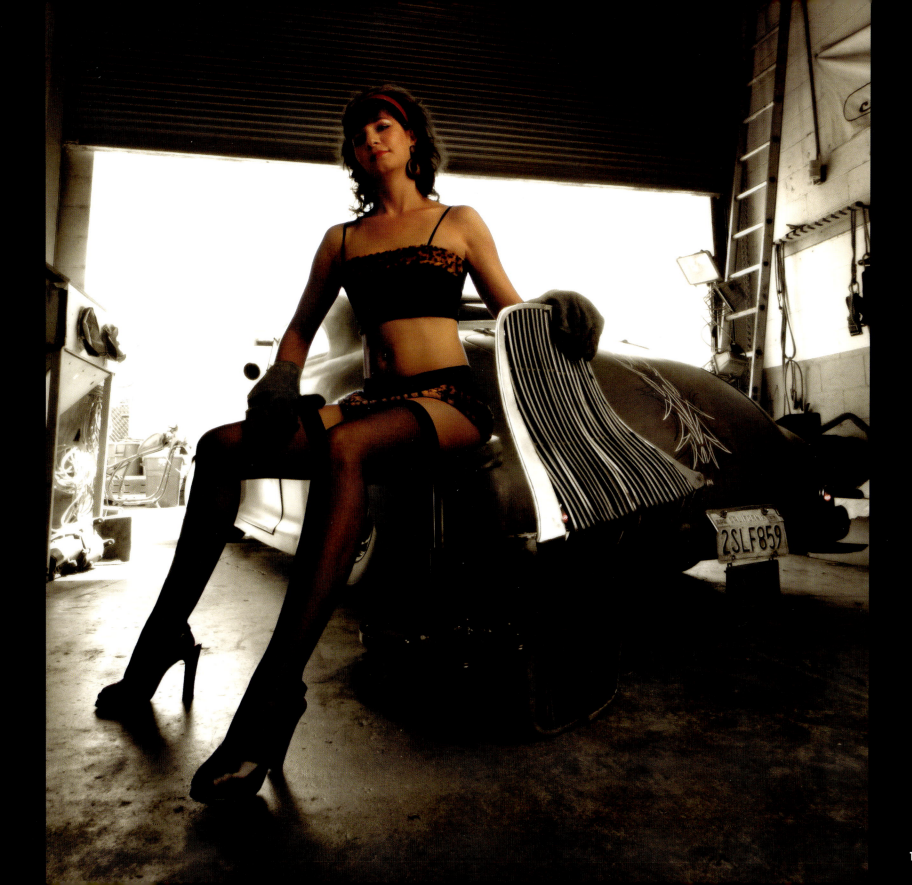

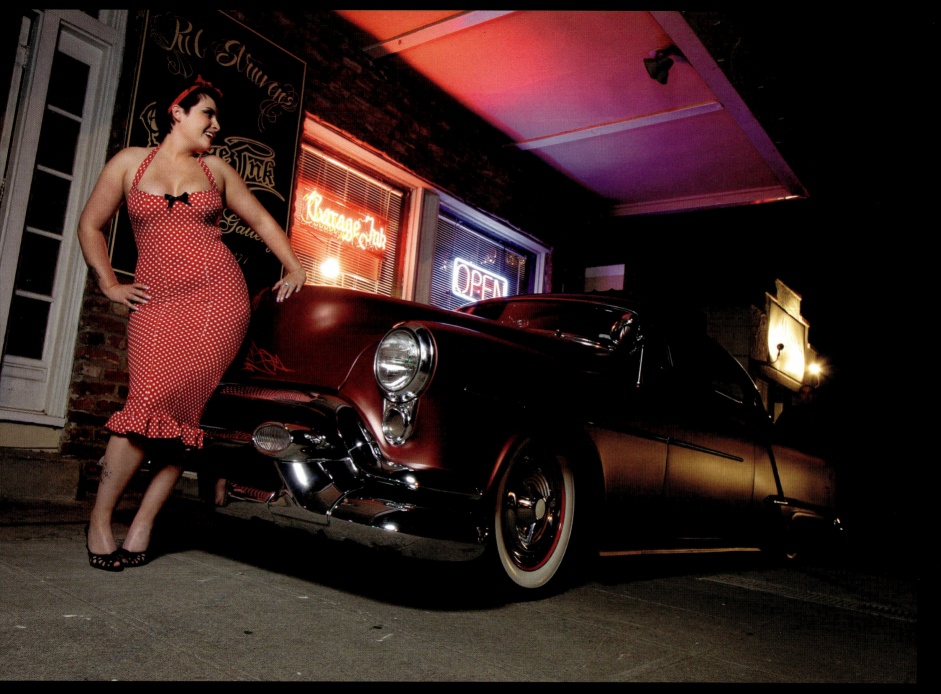

SARA   1953 Oldsmobile Rocket   Owner: Rob Struven   Club: Swanx   Location: Napa, California

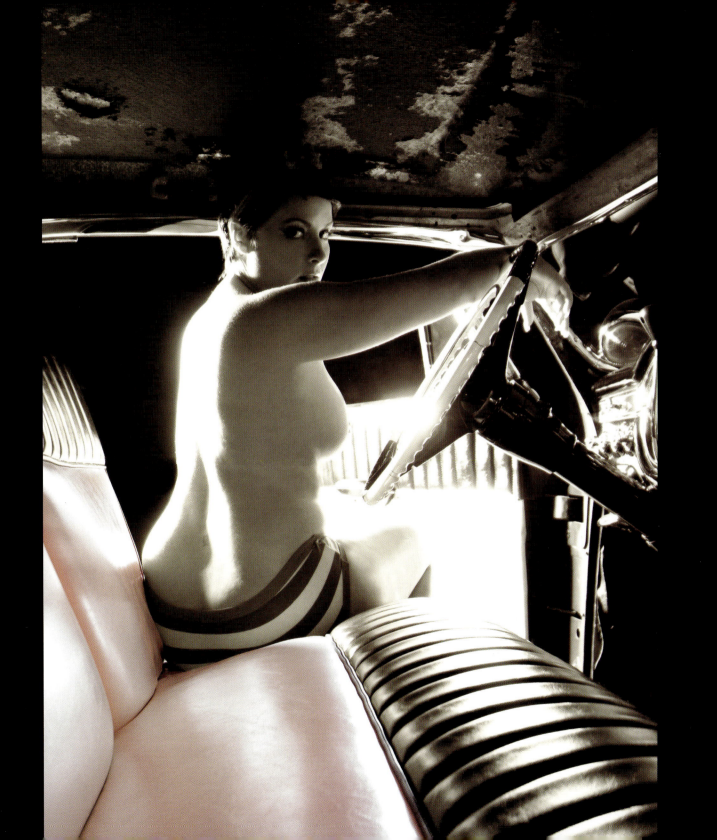

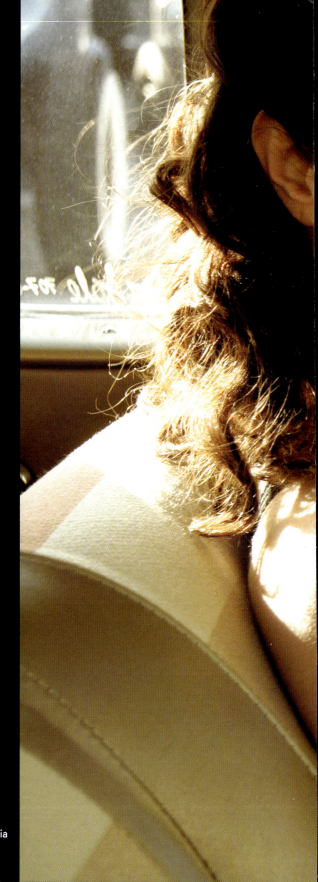

LARK | 1958 Chevy Impala | Owner: Ezio Siri | Location: Vallejo, California

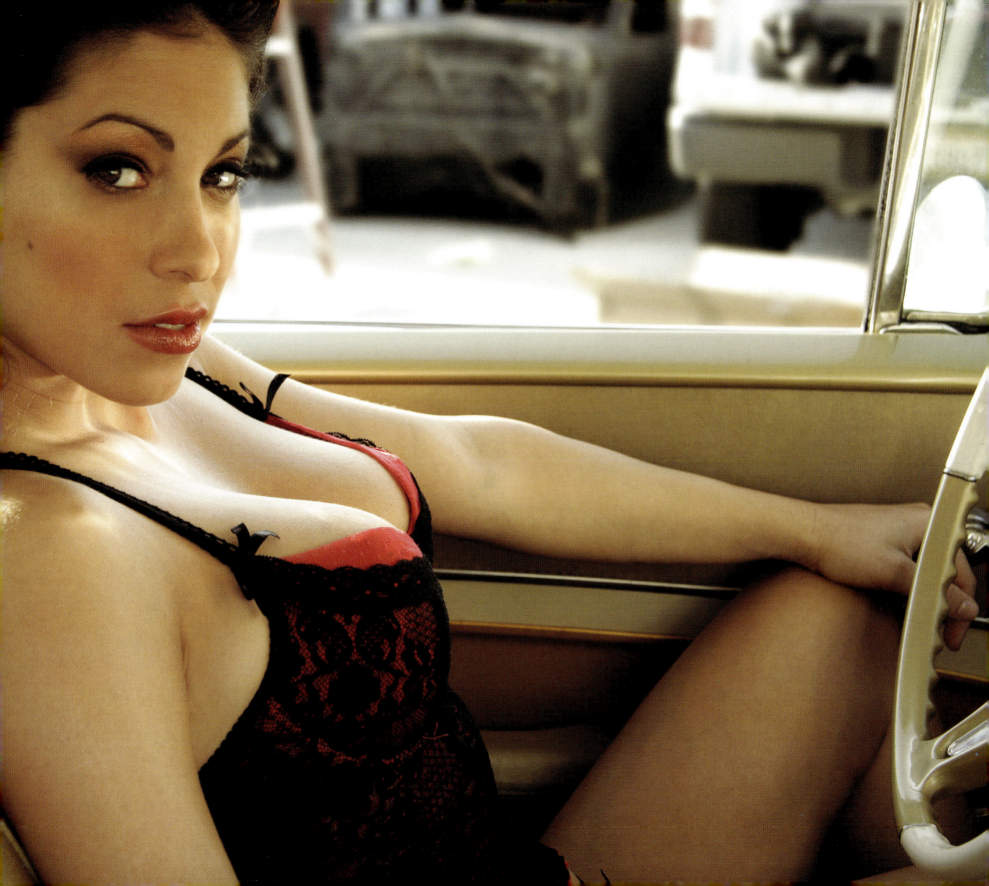

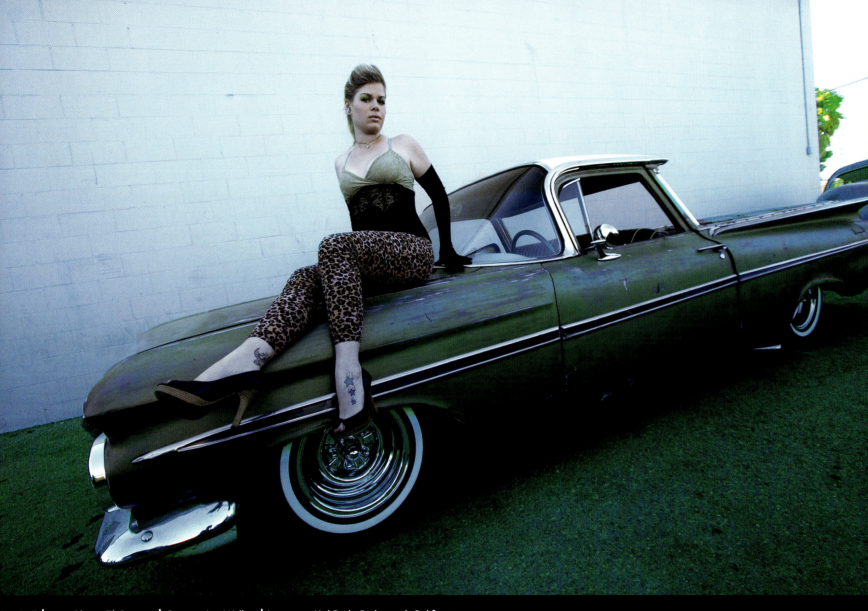

DANAE | 1959 Chevy El Camino | Owner: Joe Walker | Location: Kid Built, Richmond, California

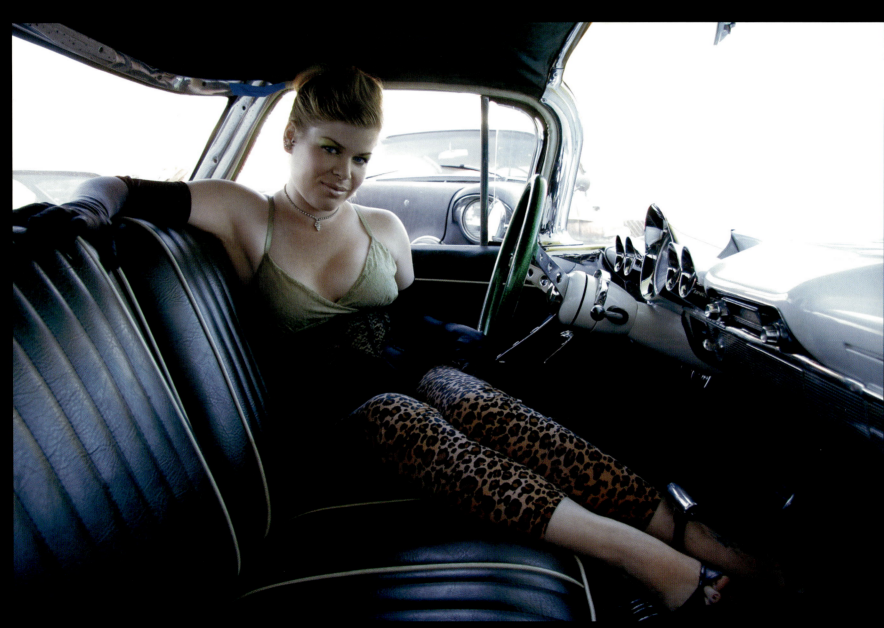

After sneakin' out of the house, delinquent damsel Danae gets caught drivin' Joe's pickup.

JAMIE | 1954 Mercury | Owner: Brent Rees | Club: Drag Lynx | Location: Auburn, California

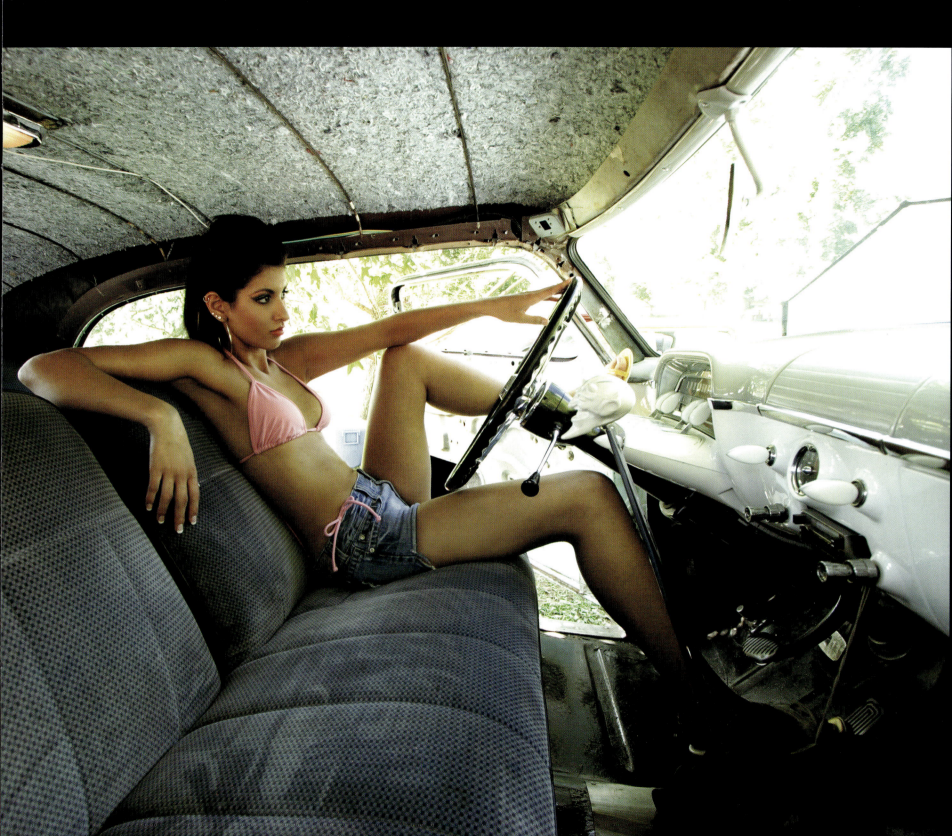

BETHANY | 1959 Chevy Bel Air Special | Owner: Andrew Podesta | Club: Villains | Location: Auburn, California

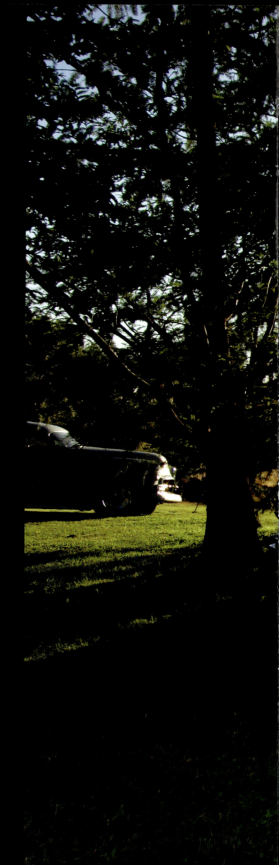

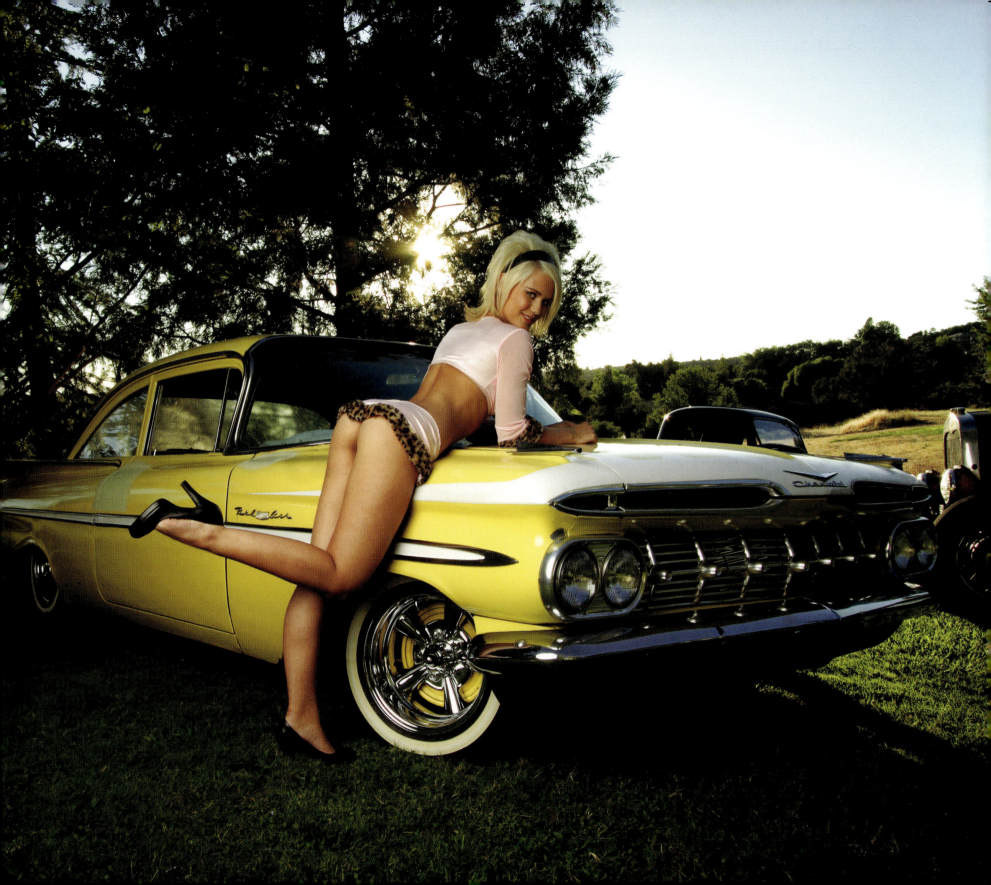

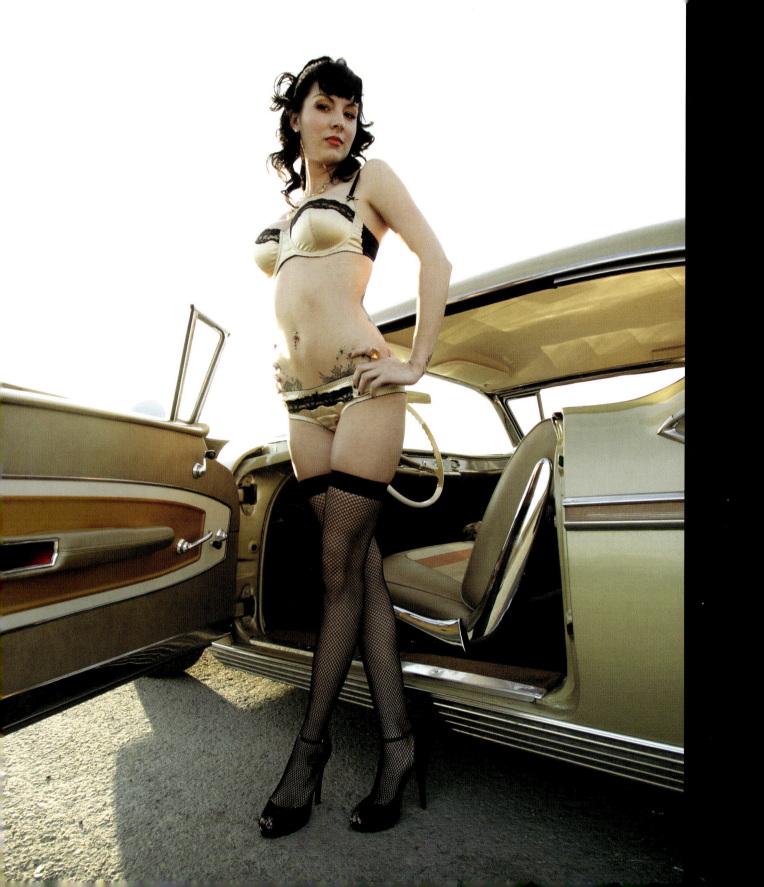

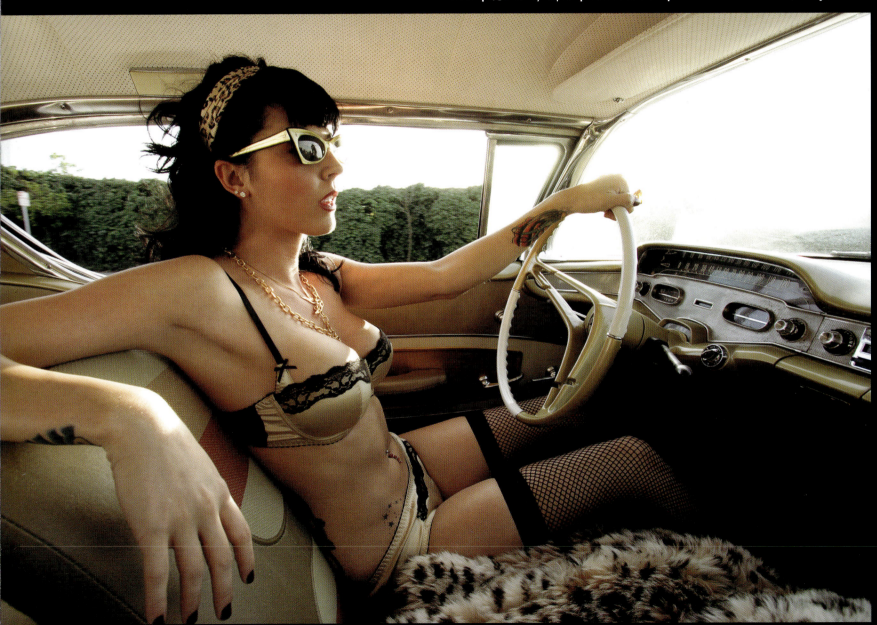

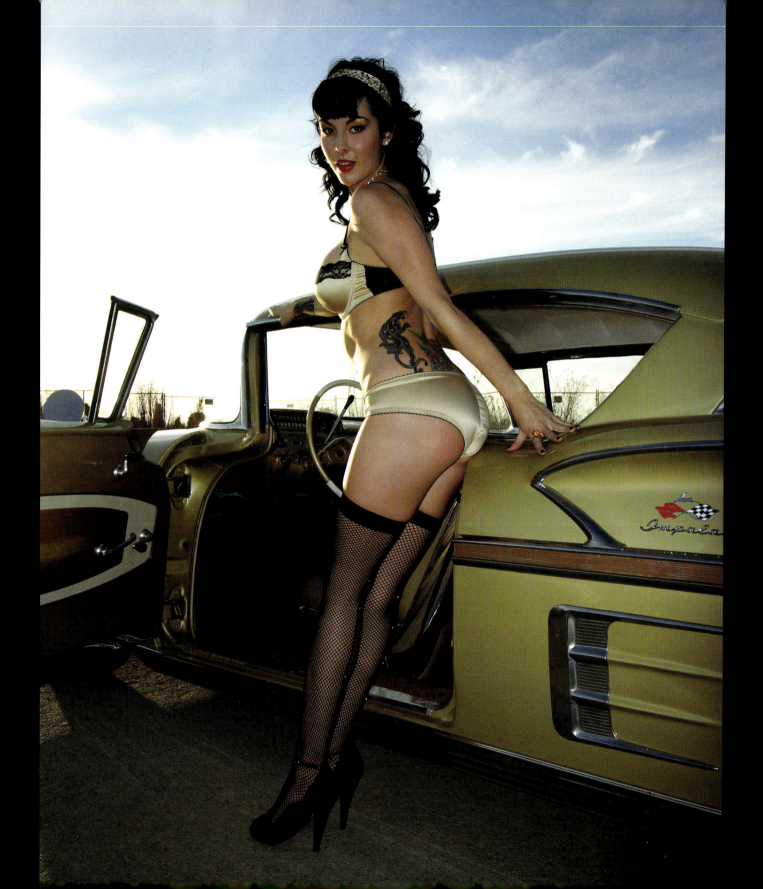

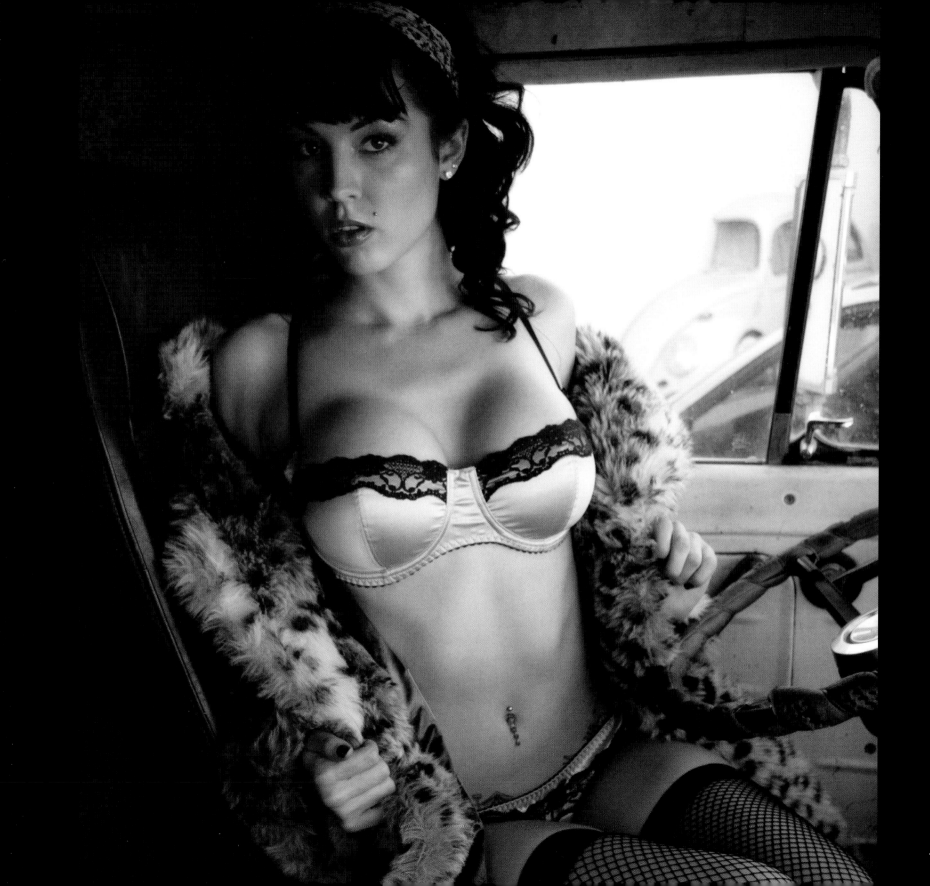

SOMEWHERE WEST OF LARAMIE

BY CHRIS SHELTON

It's popular to say *Hot Rod* founder Bob Petersen was the guy who inextricably linked hot girls with cool cars. And for good reason: the "Parts with Appeal" column that appeared on page fifteen of that first issue in 1948 was monumental.

In it, a bathing suit–clad Jane Norred brandished more than just the pumps on her feet: in her hand was another, this one for fuel. Whose pump is it? Who knows or cares! What we do know is that Ms. Norred was nineteen, lived in Culver City, and was looking for a tall and dark man with a sense of humor and who liked to ride horses.

While Petersen certainly wasn't the first to photograph a girl with a car, the "Parts with Appeal" column indeed set a precedent of sorts: half-nekkid women and cars were as natural a combination as peas and carrots. The mold was struck and has since become a staple of the automotive world.

However, this association between cars and attractive women is a few years older—twenty-five to be exact. To talk about this precursor to the "Parts with Appeal" touchstone as part of a prelude to pin-up photography probably seems a little peculiar, first for the fact that it appeared in the *Saturday Evening Post*, and second because it doesn't feature a pin-up photograph or even a traditional pin-up illustration at all. But if you subscribe to the notion that nothing is more prurient than the mind's eye, the text within the advertisement for the 1923 Jordan is as compelling as a Gypsy Rose Lee striptease. Or a Vargas painting. Or a David Perry photograph.

"Somewhere west of Laramie," it begins, "there's a broncho-busting [sic], steer-roping girl who knows what I'm talking about.

"She can tell what a sassy pony, that's a cross between greased lightning and the place where it hits, can do with eleven hundred pounds of steel and action when he's going high, wide and handsome. The truth is—the Playboy was built for her."

A car called the Playboy? For a woman? Yeah, right. The rest of the ad—which, it's worth noting, makes no mention of any of the vehicle's mechanical features—reads like a Coolidge-era *Penthouse* Forum for cowboys. It continues "... she loves the cross of the wild and the tame ... a hint of old loves—and saddle and quirt," and concludes, "... real living with the spirit of the lass who rides, lean and rangy, into the red horizon of a Wyoming twilight." I don't know about you, but I would certainly tie an onion to my belt and skip on over to Shelbyville for a piece of that!

Okay, so it sounds a bit tame by today's standards, but it was no doubt plenty randy for pre-Depression America. And randy prose was no stranger to the copywriter Ned Jordan, who also happened to be the founder of the Jordan Motor Car Company and a former advertising executive from Kenosha, Wisconsin. Three years earlier, he got his hands smacked for printing an ad for the same car in the same magazine, this one dubbed "Port of Missing Men." As you can tell by the title, he was a bit more than suggestive, and the artwork that accompanied the copy showed a Playboy car in front of a seaside cottage bereft of all light but that from the bedroom. A Playboy, indeed!

As for our girl "Somewhere West of Laramie," in 1973 Jordan told Tim Howley of *Old Cars*:

When I wrote that copy, I was a week late for the *Post* deadline. On the Overland Limited, roaring over the Wyoming Highlands, bound for San Francisco, we passed some station in Wyoming, too late to catch the sign. Just then the train slowed down. Outside was a horse acting as if he were having his first look at the Union Pacific Iron Horse. Ahh, the girl on that rarin' cayuse! Her hair was flying in the wind, and at every leap that broncho [sic] looked as if he might soar off into the wild blue yonder.

"Where are we now?" I inquired of my companion, just to make conversation.

"Oh, somewhere west of Laramie," he yawned.

I took an envelope from my pocket, wrote down the phrase, and rambled on. . . .

So why are we talking about the printed word in a book about photographs? Well, primarily because it's a safe forum to discuss the subject. Suggestive photographs are the subjects of hot-button "moral" issues, whereas suggestive words seldom are—even when they flagrantly subordinate their subjects.

Take, for example, ad copy General Motors scratched up for the '63 Cadillac. "Cadillac Ladies Love to Play Chauffeur," the title announced. Underneath, it read, "This one is really fun to drive." Which one? The Cadillac or the Cadillac Lady?

After making the case that women were merely dolls, here for men to plunder—or "drive," in this case—the company lunged forward with the following: "Quick and nimble in the clutches." In the clutches of what? An off-camber turnpike? Honestly, Cadillac no longer even had the defensive veil of a clutch by that time—its cars hadn't had one in the conventional sense in a generation.

I pick on GM, but they weren't the only ones. Earlier, Chrysler claimed of its DeSoto Division's latest, "This baby can flick its tail at anything on the road," suggesting its car could walk with a switch. And how did Mercury *not* get called on this one: "We dressed in silence. And drove. Until four lanes became two. Two became one. And one became a tunnel." A tunnel? Good God . . . they stopped just short of saying our hero was taking his gal to the submarine races! That same year, 1992, Ford beckoned us to "Go where no one has gone before . . . go farther than all the others." Why didn't they just cut to the chase and tell us that we could make it to second base in the back seat of the new Explorer? Ater all, it certainly wasn't worth a damn for anything more technical than, say, a speed bump.

Aside from being less tawdry, Ned presented his Jordan-driving Wyoming cowgirl in a pretty flattering sense: here's a woman in control, and the command she has over her environment makes her seem alluring. For a man to make a woman sound equally powerful and titillating three years after the 19th Amendment—that's the right for women to vote, sonny—is pretty powerful and rather notable if you ask me. By contrast, forty years later Cadillac made the case that women were objects, something to vanquish. Man, did we backslide or what?

Here's my point: Just as there always has been and still is a wide margin of gender depictions within the world of ad copy, there's a similarly huge one in pin-up photography. In this sense, David Perry is a cut above many of his peers. He tends to depict his subjects as sensuous partially by showing them looking powerful.

When in a car, for example, they're frequently at the helm. They wield torches and grind on metal. Others have smudged cheeks, as if to suggest they've actually *ridden* the bike they're astride. Sure, there's a bit of cheesecake in there—this is pin-up photography, after all—but refreshing in their absence are the improbable poses, the string bikinis, and the obligatory wet T-shirt.

Often what makes a David Perry pin-up so alluring is what it *doesn't* show. Take one of his most enduring shots: that of a gal holding court after what was ostensibly a successful dry lakes run. She's wearing a sports bra, and draped from her shoulders is the upper half of a fire suit. Imagine that—a girl with hair a-tangle, floating in a big puffy suit, not even posing for the camera at all, and just about every one of my gearhead friends covets her.

It's almost as if David's subjects play peek a boo, which is, in another way, to say that they're in control of the situation. In fact, some of 'em look like they could rightly kick your ass, which is pretty damn sexy, too—provided you've shed the notion that a woman in charge is threatening. I guess that says a lot about you, the viewer.

Just as Ned Jordan and Bob Petersen stuck out their necks when they made their statements in 1923 and 1948, respectively, so too does David Perry every time he presses that shutter.

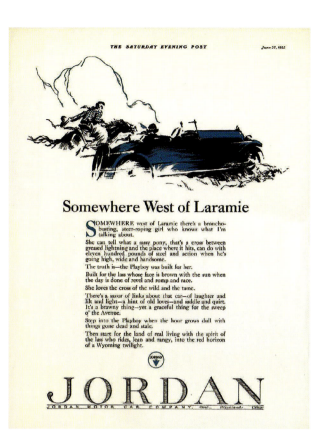

CONTRIBUTOR BIOS

The incomparable **Chris "COOP" Cooper** requires no introduction among hot rod, punk rock, and fine-art aficionados. His pacesetting art has graced posters and album art for the likes of the Mono Men, Lords of Acid, Cheater Slicks, Reverend Horton Heat, Bad Religion, Soundgarden, and several other acts (www.coopstuff.com). More recently, his seventy-eight-foot-long painting, *Parts with Appeal*, won critical acclaim in all corners of the globe. Mr. Coop also maintains a popular blog (www.positiveapeindex.blogspot.com), and he campaigned the 2006 Carrera Pan Americana.

Jim Nisbet is the author of nine novels, five volumes of poetry, and innumerable individual poems, essays, stories, and excerpts that have appeared in nearly as many newspapers, magazines, and anthologies, including this volume's predecessor, *Hot Rod Pin-ups*. A native Southerner, rehabilitated hot rodder, and Pushcart Prize nominee, Mr. Nisbet is also a maker of fine furniture for home and office. He is online at www.noirconeville.com.

Longtime hot rodder, hot rod and motorsport journalist and historian, and British expat **Tony Thacker** is the author and coauthor of several books on hot rods and customs, including *Hot Rods by Ed "Big Daddy" Roth*, *SO-CAL Speed Shop*, *Hot Rods & Custom Cars*, *Sundays with Von Dutch*, and *'32 Ford Deuce*. Mr. Thacker currently serves as executive director of the National Hot Rod Association Wally Parks Motorsports Museum in Pomona, California.

Born in Binghamton, New York, and raised on Long Island, **Kevin Thomson** migrated to Austin, Texas, to attend the University of Texas theater program. However, punk rock and skateboarding soon rendered university irrelevant, and Mr. Thomson embarked on a musical career, releasing several singles, EPs, and LPs with such outfits as Morning Champ, Touched by a Janitor, and Enablers. In 1994 he was offered a regular column in *Gearhead* magazine. Since then, his byline has also appeared in *Garage* and *Rust* magazines and in the Motorbooks titles *Hot Rod: The Photography of Peter Vincent* and *Hot Rod Pin-ups*. Mr. Thomson is also the coauthor, with Mr. Perry, of the Motorbooks bestseller *Hot Rod Kings*.

Charles Verne appears to be a *nom de plume* used by, or assigned to, the writer hired to create the 1957 hardcover *Mr. Hot Rod*, the first words of which are reproduced here. The book was rereleased by a second publisher in 1964 under the title *Hot-Rod Babe*, a seventy-five-cent paperback credited this time to Tom Haunt and featuring decidedly racier cover art. Searches of the U.S. Copyright Office and Stanford University's database of copyright renewals indicate the copyright was never renewed, rendering the fate of the publishers and author a mystery. A classic example of the J.D. genre of pulp fiction, the storyline could make the likes of Jim Thompson or Raymond Chandler blush. It features no fewer than five women vying for the attentions of the antihero, hot rodder Eric Godard. Suffice to say, none of these gals are of the poodle-skirt-and-saddle-shoe variety.

Loathe even to the *idea* of a real job, **Chris Shelton** jammed his foot into the publishing door by sweet-talking a noteworthy editor into an internship at a leading rod magazine. While Mr. Shelton's detractors attribute his uncanny success to a stack of compromising photos of editors ("Pure hogwash," he contends), his advocates sometimes praise his seemingly innate understanding of the automobile and its cultural value (even if it mortally impairs all other aspects of his life, his beleaguered wife will tell you). Whether in spite of or due to his oblique approach, Mr. Shelton's byline appears in *Street Rodder*, *Rod & Custom*, *The Rodder's Journal*, and *Garage Magazine*, to name just a few.

ACKNOWLEDGMENTS

Dennis Pernu, Suzi Hutsell, Heather Perry, Matt Seret, Lolita Girl Clothing, Bummer, Sarah, Jim and Linda, Scott Mugford, Swanx–Vallejo, Casuals–Vallejo, Vacavillians–Vacaville, the Lemon Street Gang–Vacaville, Ezio Siri, Rich Matle, Bob & Frank, David Leeroy at The Used Tire Shop, Boris Hickman and "The Hickman Hut" tiki bar, Olli Lehtinen, Timo Jämsen, Unu Vinhava, Valja Tapio, Timo Hersti, and Dick's Auto Sales and Rebuilding, Mound House, Nevada.

index

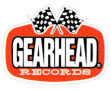
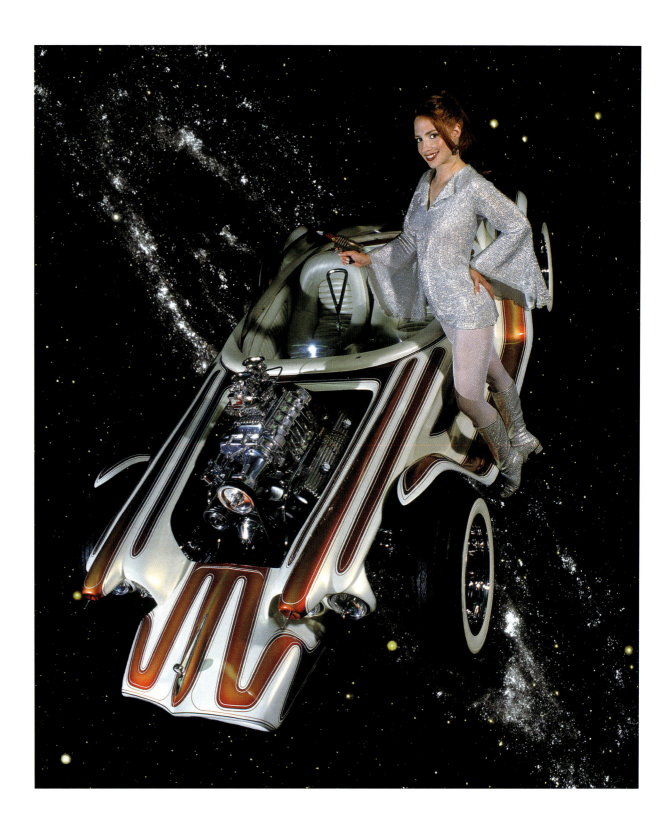

AMBER | Ed "Big Daddy" Roth's *Beatnik Bandit*
Location: National Automobile Museum, Reno, Nevada